From the library of

_____

_____

DYNAMICS FOR LIVING

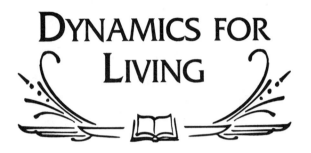

A Topical Compilation of
Essential Fillmore Teachings

Selected and Arranged by
Warren Meyer

Charles Fillmore Reference Library

UNITY® Books

Unity Village, Missouri

CONTENTS

Foreword

After three decades of studying his writings, it is my conclusion that Charles Fillmore was the greatest sage who has been embodied in the last five hundred years. His steadfast research into the realms of God Mind opened to him infinite adventures. These revelations he generously shared with all who studied in his classes or pondered over his writings. Prayer opened this man's human consciousness to the dynamics of Spirit.

I knew Charles Fillmore as a man with a diamond character. His sparkling humor, his radiant smile, and his luminescent logic quickened the atmosphere of every room he entered. His genuine humility, his simplicity of requirements, and his complete dedication to Truth were always deeply felt by everyone who was in his presence.

Prayer and faith caused him and his wife Myrtle to be the responsive instruments for a spiritual movement. What she first perceived, practiced, and proved with the healing laws of God, he examined diligently before complete acceptance. However, when he experienced the full impact of the practicality of spiritual science, the way was opened for the evolvement of the Unity movement.

On August 22, 1854, at 4 a.m., Charles Fillmore was born in a log cabin constructed on an Indian reservation near the small community of St. Cloud, Minnesota. There was no thought then, of course, that many people would be transformed by his influential teachings. But the years are proving that his consciousness of universal Truth has established a reliable cornerstone for the spiritual growth of hundreds of thousands of people.

What is "new" about this book is the arrangement in which this compilation is offered. Its purpose is to present the basic substance of Charles Fillmore's writings in a manner that will invite an expanded study of what he taught.

The sequence employed is a result of Charles Fillmore's own logical thinking trends. The various sections cover particular conceptions. Such were assembled from the various books and articles by Mr. Fillmore so that each unit would be complete in treating a specific subject.

It is my prayer that as you unfold your understanding of the truth that is so beautifully and positively stated in the following pages, you will find the same dynamics for living that graced the life of Charles Fillmore.

Warren Meyer

November 15, 1966

Invocation

I AM NOW in the presence of pure Being and immersed in the Holy Spirit of life, love, and wisdom.

I acknowledge Thy presence and Thy power, O blessed Spirit; in Thy divine wisdom now erase my mortal limitations and from Thy pure substance of love bring into manifestation my world, according to Thy perfect law.

—Charles Fillmore

Practical Christianity

PEOPLE everywhere on earth are now realizing as never before that the well-being of this world rests with its inhabitants. It is no longer a religious dogma or a philosophical theory that the destiny of the race is in the hands of man.

Humanity has built age after age only to find that its structures do not endure. They are faulty because the divine plan has not been consulted by the builder. Our Bible plainly teaches that God implanted in man executive ability to carry out all the creative plans of the Great Architect.

The great and most important issue before

the people today is the development of man's spiritual mind and through it unity with God. The taproot of all confusion is our failure to use our minds intelligently. Religion and all that it implies in prayer and recognition of God in idea and manifestation is the one and only way out of the chaos in which we find ourselves. We must therefore begin at once to develop this unity with the Father mind by incorporating divine ideas into all that we think and speak.

People in this atomic age civilization ask why God does not reveal Himself now as He did in Bible days. The fact is that God is talking to people everywhere, but they do not understand the message. We need to divest ourselves of the thought that wise men of the Bible were especially inspired by God, that they were divinely appointed by the Lord to do His work. Everything points to their spiritual insight as the result of work on their part to that end.

Thus, practical Christianity is the only system of religions before the people today that, because of its universal appeal to the pure reason in man, can be accepted and applied by everyone and every nation under the sun.

Revival   Modern metaphysics is merely a revival of the philosophies taught by an almost forgotten past. The principles that underlie existence are being again brought to the attention of men. The race is again entering the cycle of knowledge. We catch once more the light of pure reason and honest logic.

Few people have come into the light. Pure reason is almost an unknown quantity. When strict deductive methods are introduced into religion, and logical conclusions are reached from a stated premise, the average believer is at sea. People have been taught that certain relations exist arbitrarily no matter how opposed these relations may be to the logic necessary to cause and effect.

In order to arrive at a mutually harmonious and correct conclusion, the result of a logical argument, we must have a premise or point of beginning upon which we can all agree. Logic in its strictest sense is the only accurate method for arriving at truth. That system of philosophy or religious doctrine which does not admit of the rules of perfect logic in reaching its conclucions from a stated premise must be outside the pale of pure reason and in the realm of manmade dogma.

To know accurately about the reality of things we must disregard all appearances as indicated by the five senses and go into *pure reason*—the Spirit from which was created everything that has permanent existence.

The Difference   Practical Christianity and
                        Truth stand upon the
same foundation and are interchangeable terms.
Practical Christianity is not a theory having
origin in the human mind; nor is it a revelation
to humanity from some prophet whose word
alone must be taken as unquestionable authority.
It is in this respect totally different from the
other religious systems of the world because it
does not in any respect rest its authority upon
revelation. It has no dogmas nor creeds, nor are
its students expected to believe anything which
they cannot logically demonstrate to be true.

It takes as the basis of its doctrine a fundamental truth that is known alike by savage and
civilized, and from that truth, by cold, deductive
reasoning, arrives at each and every one of the
conclusions which are presented. Thus it does
not in any manner partake of the popular concept of religion, as a vague something which has
to be accepted on faith, and believed regardless
of its consistencies. On the contrary, it invites
the closest mental scrutiny. The analytical logi-
cian will find a new world open to him in following the sequential deductions which this
science of pure reasoning evolves.

Truth of the Ages   This system of deduc-
                         tions from intuitively

ascertained facts is not new, nor are its conclusions new, for the historian tells us that similar methods of arriving at the fundamental truth of things were in vogue thousands of years ago. Long before the historical period, legend and tradition report the existence of temples where pure reason was taught. History also tells of similar schools that existed five thousand years before Christ.

Faithfulness   You will find, if you are faithful in following the line of argument here presented, that a principle will be disclosed to you which will demonstrate itself in an unmistakable manner. The logical deductions from the premise stated may not come to your full comprehension at once because of certain intellectual limitations into which the race has plunged itself. Men have been so long divorced from logic and pure reason that they are confused when a clear-cut proposition is stated and carried to a conclusion along the lines of perfect sequence.

Independent Thought   To think in an independent, untrammeled way about anything is foreign to the habit of the races of the Occident. Our lines of thought and act are based upon precedent and

arbitrary authority. We boast much of our freedom and independence, but the facts are that
we defer to custom and tradition. Our whole
civilization is based upon manmade opinions.
We have never thought for ourselves in religion, consequently we do not know how to
think accurately and consecutively upon any
proposition. We have not been trained to draw
conclusions each for himself from a universal
pivotal truth. Consequently, we are not competent to pass judgment upon any statement so
predicated. Our manner of deciding whether
or not certain statements are true or false is to
apply the mental bias with which heredity, religion, or social custom has environed us, or else
fly to some manmade record as authority.

In the study of practical Christianity all such
temporary proofs of Truth are swept aside as
chaff. We entertain nothing in our statements
of Truth that does not stand the most searching
analysis, nothing that cannot be practically demonstrated.

Starting Point   In order to carry on an in-
                        telligent, rational line of
argument it is necessary to find a mutual starting
point which is universally accepted as true.
There may be many pivotal points chosen from
an intellectual standpoint that would doubtless

be accepted as reasonably true. Upon close analysis they will usually be found resting upon another and anterior so-called truth. For instance, we might agree that ponderable objects always fall toward the earth. Yet, the question quickly arises, "What causes them to fall?" The ready answer is, "Gravity, of course." "But what is gravity?" Thus, we are led back and back until lost in First Cause, or God.

In agreement upon a statement as the basis of an argument of universal nature, we must be careful to get one that has no anterior. There can be but one basis of being, and consequently but one basis of being's movements and forms. When we have fully agreed that everything of which we are cognizant can be traced in its last analysis to God, and no further, we have a basis upon which to rest a doctrine that cannot be successfully opposed, if its deductions are logical and can be demonstrated. This is exactly what is claimed for this science of Christ. It is not only a system of philosophy which cannot be disputed by the rational mind, but it also demonstrates in the world of phenomena that its conclusions are true.

Primal Cause   Having decided upon God, or Primal Cause, as the basis of our system, the next step is to decide

upon the nature of this Primal Cause. It is safe
to assert that in all the world not a single person of intelligence can be found who would say
that God is anything but good. It requires no
exhaustive reasoning to arrive at this conclusion, for it is the ready response of the intuitive
faculty of all mankind, which it is always safe
to count as correct.

Having agreed that God, or the Primal
Cause of all things, is the only safe basis on
which to predicate an argument that deals with
life in all its sinuous windings, and that the
nature of that First Cause must necessarily be
only Good, we can by logical deduction evolve
a doctrine that must of necessity be universal
in its application.

It is sometimes thought by certain people
that man should not attempt to find out the
nature of God because He is so far above and
beyond the comprehension of the finite that
such attempts are sacrilegious folly. Yet when
carefully analyzed it is found that the one aim
and end of man's existence is to find God. The
source of life is the great mystery which has
commanded the closest attention and study of
men in all ages, and as that source must be the
Infinite, it is thus ever inviting man to comprehend it.

The Bible says, "No man has ever seen

God," and our physical scientists all agree that primordial life, or First Cause, is invisible or spiritual, exhibiting itself as an intelligent force. Hence, as corollary to the statement that God, or First Cause, is *good,* we assert that He is also Spirit.

Value to Man   Having established a basis grounded in irrefutable truth, from which deductions may be drawn in an infinite number of directions, the next very natural question that presents itself is, "What good can come to man from a study of God?"

The facts are that the only good that has come to this world has been through the study of God, notwithstanding that the preponderance of that study has been of a nature to preclude the discovery of God or His mode of manifestation. People have been taught that God is a personal being who rules the universe much after the manner of an arbitrary monarch. This erroneous and contracted teaching has led to a belittlement of God in the concepts of men and they have imaged a man-god, and have also formed a "graven image" of God, who is Spirit.

The true concept of God is that He is the Intelligent Principle of the universe, and, like all principles, totally impartial in His expressions. This is the concept of God which has come to us in this awakening age. It is not new. The wise old sages of the Orient tell us that their ancestors thousands of years ago, in secret temples dedicated to the study of God, or the Primal Cause of all, found that in certain stages of high understanding, the result of systematic training, they came into such harmonious relations with this primal principle, or First Cause, that they were endowed with causing power themselves.

They did not seek God for the sake of the power over things which might thereby accrue to them, but that they might have wisdom and understanding of the good. They found that by thinking right thoughts and living unselfishly, they awakened new faculties within themselves. They sought the good, or God, and in harmony with that law by which like attracts like, the good, or God, sought them. They found that when they came into right relations with the good, they had apparently supernatural powers.

They discovered what Jesus Christ called "the kingdom of God within," and all things were thereby added unto them. They caused, so tradition and certain records say, rain or sunshine, heat or cold, and produced at will all the fruits and flowers of the field. These records state that they could also fly through the air, having acquired an understanding of that which lies back of gravity. They, in short, controlled all the so-called forces of nature by word or thought, and proved conclusively that we become like that which we study. They studied cause and became masters of the world of effects.

Transformations　　　They found that by coming into interior relations with the invisible Cause, they were moved by it to give expression both in thought and speech to certain words. When those words were so expressed by them, wonderful transformations took place in their surroundings. The conditions which they had always assumed to be impossible of variation from what are known as the laws of nature, were in the twinkling of an eye set at naught. They had always believed that sickness, decay, and death were part of an immutable law. Yet, they found that certain words, which are in harmony with the pivotal truth that First Cause, or God, is Spirit and All-Good, heal the sick, make happy the sorrowful, and fill the coffers of the poor.

They found that this invisible Principle of pure intelligence expresses itself *only* in the words or thoughts that produce happy results. They also found that the words which work such wonders in transforming their surroundings al-

ways represent those qualities which by deductive reasoning they found can originate only
with a Being or Principle of goodness.

The Real and Unreal   They not only knew
                             God as All-Good
through the intuitive faculty, but they proved
Him so by demonstrating that He responds to
those attributes *only* that are representative of
the good. Hence, these words they called words
of Truth or reality.

On the other hand, they found that certain
other words or thoughts that do not correspond
to or harmonize with the attributes of a primal
cause of good produce conditions of inharmony.
Under their expression people become sick,
sorrowful, and generally unhappy.

Through spiritual illumination, by comparison, logical deduction, and practical demonstration, they definitely arrived at words of
Truth and their opposites. They knew that the
words of Truth must proceed from the cause to
which they correspond and consequently must
be the Real. They could find no tenable point
of origin for the opposites or words of error.
Thus, they necessarily classified them as the unreal, the nothings, the dropping away from the
one Principle of the universe.

They arranged and classified their words of

reality and *unreality* as the electrician of our day classifies the positive and the negative poles of electrical action. In the realm of mind the effect of the expressed words of Truth is fully as forcible as is the positive power of the battery in the realm of electricity.

The effect of words is an exact science. It can be demonstrated as such by all who will study it assiduously. It is the science of life. Upon its understanding hinges the happiness or unhappiness of man's existence. It is not a science whose laws were discovered and arbitrarily classified by those metaphysicians of the past. On the contrary, it is universal in its unfoldment and application. Every man works in its laboratory every day of his life and is using its principles with every thought he thinks and every word he speaks. He uses the law whether he knows it or not. Hence, no one should be ignorant of the effects which the manipulation of these hidden forces produce in the character and surroundings of each child of earth.

Pure Christianity   Pure Christianity is a spiritual doctrine. It has no opposite whatsoever. In its purity it is *one* with the underlying cause of all that *is*. It admits of no differences among those who understand it. The modes of teaching it may vary, as do the characteristics of each teacher; but all its teachers must necessarily present the same Truth, though their words and illustrations may differ. Each individual needs but to be given the key in order to unlock for himself the entire metaphysical plan of the universe.

The Principle of Being is not only all good, but it is all intelligent. It is the fount of your intelligence. When you study it you will find yourself becoming one with the principle of all wisdom. To be one with the principle of All Intelligence is to *know*. When you *know* you will find yourself so broad in judgment and understanding that you will have charity for all who differ from you in religion, metaphysics, and even politics.

This system of metaphysics is but another name for universal Truth. It consequently covers the therapeutic, ethical, and religious departments of life.

Therapeutics Metaphysical therapeutics treats of healing by an understanding of the reality of things. It does not in its exact meaning teach how to heal diseases by the power of thought. It teaches how, by the power of thought, false conceptions may be eradicated and the divine Reality brought into manifestation, showing forth in health and harmony. This department attracts the majority of people because of the great need of healing.

Ethics   Ethics in the curriculum of metaphysics shows the student how the moral world may be reformed. It teaches him how he may be wise and happy by holding in mind certain thoughts that will bring about these conditions. It shows him how he may attain his ideal ends in reforming society. It shows him how a dull, stupid, or ignorant mind may be quickened morally and brightened intellectually by the power of right thinking.

Religion   The religion of metaphysics includes all these and adds to them a certain and sure knowledge of man's immortality and divine relation. The religion of metaphysics is its crowning principle—it is this department that places it in the category of science. Religion is a science—the science of life. It will so demonstrate itself to the student, both logically and practically.

When you understand it in its religious aspect you know your true relation to the Creator, and just what that relation must lead to. You get a revelation of your status as a living soul that is impregnable in its logic, and you are brought into such close relation with the divine

Cause that you know intuitively that you are
not of the flesh, but of God.

Upliftment   Nothing is too small or in-
                    significant for God's uplift-
ing presence. God is not a theory of life. He is
life itself. He is the harmonious manifestation
of life.

Those who have honestly studied metaphysics and applied its rules in their daily work will
tell you that it has made them over physically,
mentally, and morally. They will tell you that
they are better men and women; that life has
new zest for them, and that they can now do
good and help others where before they were
helpless.

New and Old   Some will tell you that they
                     were not able to make this
science fit into their old theories and incoherent
vagaries in matters religious and ethical. They
will tell you that its very simplicity stood in the
way of their quick acquirement of its power.
They had listened all their lives to learned and
ponderous disquisitions of professors upon the
body and mind, man's relation to his Maker,
etc., and had long ago decided that only the
very learned could ever hope to fathom the
depths of wisdom necessary to comprehend even

a very little of the subject. They will also tell you that from childhood they have listened to flowery sermons by learned ministers about God and man's duty to Him. Yet in all this, the subjects were so encumbered with the ponderous appearance of wisdom that they failed to connect them with simple, everyday life.

Here we have a presentation of the deep things of God, so simple and easy that the wise and mighty pass it by as a religious vagary.

Problems of Life   The problem of life is getting into more and more of a tangle among those who depend upon the material. There is much running to and fro upon the earth by seekers for satisfaction, yet no satisfaction is found.

Where will you find a person who will admit that he has peace of mind, health of body, and a knowledge of Truth? The rich admit that their possessions bring increased cares and great mental disquietude. The poor long to be rich, not knowing that happiness cannot be bought with money. The learned are not satisfied with their acquirements because when they just begin to get wisdom their bodies fail them. So it goes among the denizens of this discontented world of matter. Many lose faith in things ever being better.

Happiness Here and Now   Happiness here
                                and now is the
beautiful part of Jesus' teaching. He did not
defer health nor salvation to a world to come
after death, but taught that it was attainable
right here. He taught that the kingdom of
heaven is within you. He proved by His works
that it could be made to show forth in the bodies
and minds of those who follow the way He
pointed out.

Unprejudiced Mind   If you would get
                          Truth in its purity
you must listen to its statements with the unprejudiced mind of the child. All about you are
potencies and power of which you do not dream.
Your philosophy has not grasped the faintest
concept of the wonderful, undiscovered country
that lies right within your reach, yet unseen and
unknown to the mortal senses because of their
narrow range.

    You live, move, and have your being in a
realm elysian. Now and then you may catch
faint glimpses of its rare beauty in your high
moments of spiritual illumination. This realm
is not of matter but of Mind. It encompasses
you on every side and you contact its invisible
glories, but know them not. A false education
has shut you away from God's creation.

Do you say this is idealism? The illusions of imagination?

Here again you betray the mental congealing which hereditary prejudices and race education have produced. Did not that subtle fluid, electricity, exist in the invisible before it was brought into manifestation? Does not the modern analytical chemist tell us that our planetary atmosphere carries in solution all the elements that go to make up this visible world? It is rash for any man to assert that anything is impossible.

New Era   A new era has dawned. The old is passing away. In the advent of this new dispensation the heavens are rolled up as a scroll, and in that process is revealed the long-hidden realm of causes. Invisible forces are always the most powerful. The dynamics of mind control the universe. In mind originates all that is. By its actions all things are moved. When man understands the laws of mind he has solved the mysteries of the universe.

The New Testament is a sealed book to one who has no knowledge of the laws of mind. It is a secret manual. It reads like an ordinary narrative unless one has the key that unlocks its hidden meaning.

Practical Christianity gives that key. He who knows all the principles of its philosophy can enter the holy of holies of the Bible. He can penetrate the mysteries of the sacred scriptures of all peoples. There is no limit as to time, place, or personality in Scriptural promises.

Study of Truth   In the study of Truth you are not under any circumstances to listen to testimony of your external senses. You are placed in the clear light of logic and reason, and are expected to draw all of your conclusions from that standpoint. From the premise of Spirit alone you shall evolve the world of reality in which you live, and you can demonstrate to your full satisfaction that you have been deluded all these years in believing that which is not true. You shall prove each for himself that all causation is from Spirit, that you can make the world in which you live conform to that which you know by clear reason to be true.

The one Life-Intelligence is your life-intelligence. When you let it freely flow into your consciousness, you know that it is all good. As there can be but one Cause for all that is, and as that Cause is All-Good, you have a pivotal center from which you can draw conclusions that will settle definitely all the debatable questions of existence.

God

THE starting point in spiritual realization is a right understanding of God. By describing God with words in our human way we are but stating in the lisping syllables of the child that which in its maturity the mind still only faintly grasps. Words never express that which God is. Language is the limitation of mind. Do not expect the unlimited to leap forth into full expression through the limited. We must drop the complex and find simplicity before we can know God. We must become as a child.

Being   God's name represents wholeness.
               He is holy, perfect. God is Being;
the Creator; the Infinite; the Eternal; the Ruler
of the universe. Being is omnipresent, omnipotent, omniscient; it is the fullness of God. God
is the absolute, incomparable, omnipresent All-
Good, the principle of divine benevolence that
permeates the universe. Being exists under two
phases: invisible and visible, abstract and concrete. The visible comes forth from the invisible,
and this coming forth is always according to a
universal method of growth. From center to
circumference is the plan of procedure throughout the universe.

Principle   We must relieve our minds of
                a personal God ruling over us
in an arbitrary, manlike manner. God is not person but Principle. By Principle is meant definite,
exact, unchangeable. It best describes the un-
changeableness that is an inherent law of Being. The fundamental basis of practical Christianity is that God is Principle.

Divine Principle is fundamental Truth. God
as Principle is the unchangeable life, love, intelligence, and substance of Being. It is the underlying plan by which God moves in expressing Himself. Principle does not occupy space;
neither has it any limitations of time or matter,

but it eternally exists as the underlying cause out of which come forth all true ideas. Although Principle is formless, it is that by which all form is produced. God immanent in the universe is the great underlying Cause of all manifestation; the Source from which form proceeds.

Law   God as law is Principle in action. Everything has its foundation in a rule of action, a law. Divine law is the orderly working out of the principles of Being. Divine law cannot be broken. It places first things first. Divine order is the first law of the universe. Indeed, there could be no universe unless its various parts were kept in perfect order.

Reality   God is the one harmonious Principle underlying all being and the Reality out of which all that is eternal comes. Reality is that which is abiding, eternal, and unchangeable. The basic principles of mathematics and music are real, because they are not subject to change.

Spirit   God is Spirit, the Principle of creative life, the moving force in the universe, the omnipotent, omnipresent essence from which all things proceed. God is life. God is in the universe as its constant "breath." Life

is a principle that is made manifest in living.
Spirit is not matter. Spirit is not person. Spirit
cannot be analyzed by the senses. It is beyond
their grasp. In order to perceive the essence of
Being we must drop from mind the belief that
God is circumscribed in any way or has any of
the limitations usually ascribed to persons,
things, or anything having form or shape. As the
animating life of all things God is a unit, but
as the Mind that drives this life He is diverse.

Spiritual-Science   The only real science is
                             the science of Spirit. It
never changes. By science we mean the systematic and orderly arrangement of knowledge.
Orderliness is law, and is the test of true science.
The facts of Spirit are of a spiritual character
and, when understood in their right relation,
they are orderly. The lawful truths of Spirit are
more scientific than the constantly shifting
opinions based on intellectual standards.

Mind   By the term *Mind,* we mean God—
                the universal Principle, which in-
cludes all principles. In our talk about Mind
we are forced to leave the plane of things
formed and enter the realm of pure knowing.
God is the original Mind in which all real ideas
exist. The Mind of the universe is composed of

archetype ideas: life, love, wisdom, substance, truth, power, peace, and so forth. The one original Mind creates by thought. The science of Truth is God thinking out creation.

Truth   God as Truth is the eternal verity of the universe. He is the underlying, unchangeable Truth. The absolute Truth is that which accords with God as divine Principle; that which is, has been, and ever will be; that which eternally is. The Truth of God is reality. The verities of Being are eternal.

Omnipresence   God as omnipresence is the only presence in the universe. This refers to the all-pervading presence of God, permeating the universe. God is everywhere present. There is no place where God is not. He is in all, through all, and around all.

Omnipotence   God is All-Power, all the power there is. God as omnipotence is infinite power, the Almighty. All things are possible with God, because He is infinitely all-mighty, having all power or force to accomplish anything. All the power, all the force, all the might of the universe are God's. He is, in truth, Almighty God. Spiritual power is omnipresent.

Omniscience   God as omniscience is all-
                       knowing, all knowledge.
God is Mind. God is omnipresent Mind en-
folding and interpenetrating all things. Mind
is common to all, above and below, within and
without. God must be in His universe as every-
where-intelligent power; otherwise it would
fall to pieces.

Substance   God is substance. This does not
                       mean matter. Matter is formed
while God is the formless. This substance which
God is lies back of all matter and all forms.
Substance is the divine idea of the underlying
reality of all things. Substance is everywhere
present, pervades all things. Through substance
all the attributes of Being are expressed. It
sustains and enriches any idea that is projected
into it. Divine substance is supply. It is that
which is the basis of all form yet enters not into
any form as finality. It cannot be seen, tasted, or
touched. Yet, it is the only "substantial" substance in the universe. God as substance is the
all-providing law which supplies bountifully
out of His own abundance.

Ideas   The real of the universe is held in
               the Mind of Being as ideas. The
firstborn of everything in the universe is an

idea in Divine Mind. In God Mind an idea is the eternal Word or Logos, the original, primary, or unlimited thought of Being. Ideas may be combined in a multitude of ways, producing infinite variety in the realm of forms. There is a right combination which constitutes the divine order.

Love   Love, in Divine Mind, is the idea of universal unity. Of all the attributes of God, love is undoubtedly the most beautiful. Love is the power that joins and binds in divine harmony the universe and everything in it. Divine love is impersonal; it loves for the sake of loving. Love is the great harmonizer.

Creation

The Key   On every hand men are earnestly seeking to know about God, and the origin of both the universe and themselves. They have probed with more or less success nearly every secret of nature, but of the origin of life they know comparatively nothing. A right understanding of Divine Mind is the one and only logical key. When man clearly discerns the science of Mind, he will solve easily all the mysteries of creation. To understand the creation of the universe by God, we must know something of the character of God.

Holy Trinity   The Holy Trinity is known
                   as the Father, the Son, and
Holy Spirit. Metaphysically, we understand the
Trinity to refer to mind, idea, and expression,
or thinker, thought, and action. These three are
one fundamental Mind in its three creative
aspects.

Father   Father is first in the Trinity. Father
             is Being in the absolute, the un-
limited, the unrelated. He is the Source, Origin,
Essence, Root, Principle, Law, Spirit, All-Good,
Creator of all. Father is the name of the all-
encompassing Mind, everywhere present, forever accessible. The universal Principle of Being (Elohim God) designed all creation. Elohim is God in His capacity as creative power.
Create means *ideate*. Elohim creates the spiritual
idea which is afterward made manifest. God
created not the earth as it appears but that which
produced the earth.

Son   The second in the Trinity is the Son.
          It is called Jehovah [Lord] in the Old
Testament and Christ in the New Testament.
The Son of God is the fullness of the perfect-
man idea in Divine Mind. He is the man that
God created in His image. The Son is Principle
revealed in a creative plan. He is that which

proceeds from, is begotten of the Father, like Him in nature, and essentially all that the Father is. The Son ever exists in God. Father and Son are one and are omnipresent in the universe.

Christe   Christ is the one and only complete ideal man in the mind of the everywhere present God, the "only Son" of God. He is the divine-idea man. He is all divine ideas, such as intelligence, life, love, substance, and so forth. In the architect's mind there may be one masterpiece, but that masterpiece is the sum of all the beautiful ideas that have come to his mind. Christ is the cosmic or Grand Man of the universe. Christ is the name of the all-loving Mind.

The Word   The Son is also called the Logos, the Word, the anointed One, and the I AM. He is the living Word. The Logos is the Word of God; the divine archetype ideas that contains all ideas. This supreme idea is the creative power formulated by universal Principle. The law of the Logos is the law of divine creation. It produces the order and harmony of perfect thought. Law puts first things first. It is a rule of action. An understanding of the Logos reveals to us the law under which all things are brought forth, the law of mind action. Divine Mind creates by thought, through ideas.

I Am   The Son is the I AM identity of Being. I AM is eternal, without beginning or ending: the true spiritual man whom God made. Its home is in the realm of God ideals.

Holy Spirit   The Holy Spirit is just what the name implies, the whole Spirit of God in action. It is God's word in movement: the working, moving, breathing, brooding Spirit. Holy Spirit is the all-active manifestation. It is the executive power of both Father and Son, carrying out the creative plan. The Holy Spirit is the law of God in action; in that action He appears as having individuality. It is the personality of Being. It is neither the all of Being nor the fullness of Christ, but is an emanation, or breath, sent forth to do a definite work. Creation is carried forward through the activity of the Holy Spirit.

Creative Process   Creation is the original plan of an idea in Divine Mind. In the creative process Divine Mind ideates itself. God creates and moves creation through the power of Mind, through His idea or word, the universal creative vehicle. The vehicles of Mind are thoughts (ideas). God is thinking the universe into manifestation right now. Creation takes place through the operation of the Logos. The creations of the Logos are always spiritual, permanent, and incorruptible. The creative processes of Mind are continuously operative; creation is going on all the time, but the original plan, the design of Divine Mind, is finished. The processes of Mind enter into all creations. God is eternally in His creation and never separate from it. Wherever there is evidence of creative action, there God is. His avenues of expression run in every direction.

Creative Law   The order of creation is from the formless to the formed, from the invisible to the visible. This goes on perpetually and there is never a beginning or an ending to the process. The law of divine creation is perfect order and harmony. God cannot create without law. God is the Mind force carrying forward creation under law. First is Mind; then the idea Mind; then the materialization of the idea. Apart from Mind nothing can be done. Creative intelligence forever upbuilds God's universe.

Involution and Evolution   All of God's works are created in Mind as perfect ideas. He creates the ideas that form the things. The starting point of every form is an idea. This is involution. Then the ideas are made into form and shape. This is evolution. Evolution is the working out in manifestation of what Mind has involved. Whatever Mind commands to be brought forth will be brought forth by and through the law of evolution inherent in Being. This applies to the great and the small. In Mind there is but one.

Ideation   God-Mind expresses His ideas perfectly, so that there is no occasion for them to change. He images His ideas definitely and in every detail. Divine idealism is God's standard of perfection. The ideal is continually pouring itself into its creation and lifting it high and yet higher. Divine motherhood is the brooding, nourishing element of Divine Mind in which spiritual ideals are brought to fruition. The idea is the directing and controlling power. It precedes the fulfillment.

Ideation Formed   Ideas are productive and bring forth after their kind. Every idea has a specific function to perform. Every idea makes a structure after its own

image and likeness, and all such ideas and
structures are grouped and associated according
to their offices. All things rest on ideas. The idea
back of the flower is beauty. The idea back of
music is harmony. The idea back of day is light
or the dispensation of intelligence.

Man

MAN IS an idea in Divine Mind. He is the epitome of Being. Man is the apex of God's creation, created in His image-likeness. Ideal man is the perfect man, the Christ, the offspring of Divine Mind. Before there could be a man there must have been an idea of man. God, the Father, Divine Mind, had an idea of man, and this idea is his Son, the perfect-man idea, the offspring of God-Mind. This Son is the Christ, the only begotten of the Father. The Son, being the expressed image-likeness of the

Father, is perfect, even as the Father is perfect. All that we find in Divine Mind we find in its offspring.

Manifest Man   Manifest man should be as the ideal. He will be when the individual identifies himself with the Christ. When he is identified with anything less than perfection he manifests some degree of imperfection.

Man makes his world through the activity of ideas in his consciousness. The realm man is the embodiment of God. All the God-substance and the power to make it active is inherent within him.

Image-Likeness   When we are quickened to spiritual understanding and fully realize the true character of God and our own nature as the image, or idea, of God we will begin to live as Jesus lived in order that we may bring forth the likeness. To perceive the true character of God and His attributes and then to grasp our relationship to Him is to realize that His attributes are our attributes. His power is our power. His character is our character.

Man is not limited in life. He has existed with the Father always. At the very beginning of creation he was born into being through the Son, the Christ, the perfect, ideal man.

Three Departments of Man

Every man asks the question at some time, "What am I?" God answers: "Spiritually you are My idea of Myself as I see Myself in the ideal; physically you are the law of My mind executing that idea." Know yourself as an integral idea in Divine Mind. The mind of God is Spirit, soul, body; that is, mind, idea, expression. The mind of man is Spirit, soul, body—not separate from God-Mind, but existing in it and making it manifest in an identity peculiar to the individual.

Every man is building into his consciousness the three departments of God-Mind, and his success in the process is evidenced by the harmony, in his consciousness, of Spirit, soul, and body. If he is all body, he is but one-third expressed. If to body he had added soul, he is two-thirds man. If to these two he is adding Spirit, he is on the way to the perfect manhood that God designed.

Man has neither Spirit, soul, nor body of his own—he has identity only. He can say "I." He uses God Spirit, God soul, and God body, as his "I" elects. If he uses them with the idea that they belong to him, he develops selfishness, which limits his capacity and dwarfs his product. In his right relation, man is the inlet and the outlet of an everywhere-present life, substance, and intelligence. It is imperative that the individual understand this relation in order to grow naturally. Conscious identification must prevail in the whole man before he can be in right relation. This involves not only a recognition of the universal intelligence, life, and substance, but also their various combinations in man's consciousness.

Spirit-Man   Spirit in man is the I AM, the individuality. The individuality is the true self; that which is undivided from God; our spiritual identity; the God part of us. It is that which characterizes one as a distinct entity or particular manifestation of divine Principle. Individuality is eternal. It can never be destroyed. Spirit is the seat of power. Its abode is on the invisible side of man's nature. The I AM is the name of the spiritual self. I AM is man's self-identity, the center around which man's system revolves. It is established in Principle. It is divinely guided in its acts and they are in harmony with divine law. Spirit is the same in character as God. The Spirit is the divine center in man and is always in the Absolute; it does not become involved in effects but stands as the creative Cause of the absolute good. It is the indwelling Christ or spiritual nucleus within each individual.

Soul-Man   The soul is man's consciousness. It is the underlying idea back of any expression. In man, the soul is the many accumulated ideas of his present expression. In its original and true sense, the soul of man is the expressed idea of man in Divine Mind. It is that which man has apprehended or developed out of Spirit. The soul is not of the realm of God ideas but is the second emanation in the creative law. The soul touches both the inner realm of Spirit, from which it receives direct inspiration, and the external world, from which it receives impressions.

Body-Man   The body of man is soul expressing. Soul makes the body. It is the outer expression of the soul, or consciousness. The body is the precipitation of the thinking part of man. God created the idea of the body of man as a self-perpetuating, self-renewing organism which man reconstructs into his personal body. God creates the body idea, or divine idea, and man, by his thinking, makes it manifest. All thoughts and ideas embody themselves according to their character. Material thoughts make a material body. Spiritual thoughts make a spiritual body. The body is the outer court of the soul, an exact representative in form of the ideals that are revolving in the inner realms of its domain.

Consciousness

CONSCIOUSNESS is the sense of aware-
ness, of knowing. It is our knowing that
we know. The ideas that are held in mind are
the basis of all consciousness. The nature of the
ideas upon which consciousness is formed gives
character to it. Consciousness is the knowledge
or realization of any idea, object, or condition.
It is the sum total of all ideas accumulated in
and affecting man's present being. It is the com-
posite of ideas, thoughts, emotions, sensation,
and knowledge that makes up the conscious,
subconscious, and superconscious phases of
mind. It includes all that man is aware of in

spirit, soul, and body. The total consciousness of man is the conscious, subconscious, and superconscious, phases of mind working as a whole, as a unity. The harmonious working together of these three is necessary to the bringing forth of the latent possibilities of man.

Superconsciousness   The superconscious mind, Christ consciousness or spiritual consciousness, is a state that is based on true ideas, upon an understanding and realization of spiritual Truth. It is man's only sure guide through the maze of the creative process. By trusting to the infallibility of this guide, man opens himself to the inspiration of the Almighty. This phase of mind is built in accordance with the Christ ideal, or in absolute relationship to the Father. It is the perfect mind.

Conscious Mind   We are all well acquainted with the conscious mind. Through its use we establish our relations with the outer realm and recognize our individual entities. The conscious mind makes one know of one's mental operations. It is that phase of mind in which one is actively aware of one's thoughts. It is the mind through which man establishes his identity. The conscious mind should look ever to the superconscious for all direction and instruction. The Spirit of wisdom rests in the superconscious.

Subconsciousness   The subconscious mind, or subjective consciousness, is the sum of all man's past thinking. It may be called memory. The subconscious mind has no power to do original thinking. It acts upon what is given it through the conscious or the superconscious mind. All our involuntary, or automatic, activities are of the subconscious. They are the result of our having trained ourself by the conscious mind to form certain habits and do certain things without having to center our thought upon them consciously.

The subconscious is the vast, silent realm that lies back of the conscious mind and between it and the superconscious. It may be called the sensitive place of mind. Its true office is to receive impressions from the superconsciousness and to reproduce them upon the canvas of the conscious mind.

Man, however, having lost the consciousness of the indwelling Father as an ever-present reality, has reversed the process and impresses the subconscious from the conscious mind. In this way the former is made to register impressions according to the thought held in conscious mind at the time the impression is made.

It is the purpose and the nature of the sub-conscious mind to reproduce.

Twelve Centers   Inherent in the Mind of
                            Being are twelve funda-
mental ideas, which in action appear as primal
creative forces. It is possible, for man to ally
himself with and to use these original forces,
and thereby cooperate with the creative law. In
order to do this he must detach himself from
the outer forces and enter into the consciousness
of the idea lying back of them.

Man has twelve great centers of consciousness. They are centers of action. Each of these
has control of a certain function in mind and
body, in soul and body. These twelve powers are
all expressed and developed under the guidance
of Divine Mind.

You must keep the equipoise. You must in
all the bringing forth of the twelve realize that
they come from God. They are directed by the
Word of God. The twelve centers are: faith,
strength, judgment, love, power, imagination,
understanding, will, order, zeal, renunciation
(or elimination), and life.

Faith   Faith is the perceiving power of the
               mind linked with the power to shape
substance. It is spiritual assurance. It is the

power to do the seemingly impossible. It is a magnetic power that draws unto us our heart's desire from the invisible spiritual substance. Faith is a deep inner knowing that that which is sought is already ours for the taking.

Faith is the foundation of all that man does. It is closely related to the enduring, firm, unyielding forms of substance. The development of it is a key to spiritual realization. Faith in God is the substance of existence. To have faith in God is to have the faith of God. We must have faith in God as our Father and source of all the good we desire.

Faith is more than mere belief. It is the very substance of that which is believed. Faith working in spiritual substance accomplishes all things. This is the faith that cooperates with creative law. When it is exercised deep in spiritual consciousness, it finds its abode. Here it works under divine law, without variation. It brings results that are seemingly miraculous.

An understanding faith functions from Principle. It is based on knowledge of Truth. It understands the law of mind action. Therefore, it has great strength. To know that certain causes produce certain results gives a bedrock foundation for faith.

The term *blind faith* is an instinctive trust

in a power higher than ourselves. Because blind faith does not understand the principles of Being, it is liable to discouragement and disappointment.

Strength   Strength is the energy of God. In man it causes freedom from weakness; stability of character; power to withstand temptation; capacity to accomplish. Strength is physical, mental, and spiritual. All strength originates in Spirit. Strength and faith are brothers in the mind. When this bond of unity is established it carries one along, even though one may encounter the most adverse experiences.

Judgment   Judgment is a faculty of the mind that can be exercised in two ways—from sense perception or spiritual understanding. If its action be based on sense perception its conclusions are fallible and often condemnatory. If based on spiritual understanding, they are safe. Judgment is a mental act of evaluation through comparison or contrast. Spiritual discernment is the inner voice through whose expression we come into a larger realization of ourselves. We also call this faculty discrimination. It is that quality in us which carefully weighs a question and draws a conclusion.

The prevailing tendency of judgment is toward caution, fearfulness, criticism, and condemnation, when it draws its conclusions from the effect side of existence. We should therefore faithfully seek the spiritual aspect of this faculty, the guidance and good judgment of spiritual light and understanding.

Wisdom, justice, judgment are grouped under one head in spiritual consciousness. Intuition, judgment, wisdom, justice, discernment, pure knowing, and profound understanding are natural to man. All these qualities, and many more, belong to every one of us by and through his divine sonship.

Love   Love is an inner quality that sees good everywhere and in everybody. It insists that all is good, and by refusing to see anything but good it causes that quality finally to appear uppermost in itself, and in all things. Divine love will bring your own to you, adjust all misunderstandings, and make your life and affairs healthy, happy, harmonious, and free. Like the sun, its joy is in the shining forth of its nature.

Love is a divine attribute. It is an idea in the one Mind, a quality in Being. The difference between divine love and human love is that divine love is broad and unlimited, a universal and harmonizing power. Human love is based on personality. When man expresses divine love in limited ways he makes a separation in consciousness and his expression of love is personal instead of universal. When love is established in the consciousness it will draw to us all that we require to make us happy and contented, all that really belongs to us. Unselfish love is fearless, because of its forgetfulness of self. A sense of oneness is a natural product of love. It is accompanied by a consciousness of security.

Power   Man is the power of God in action. The mind and the body of man have power to transform energy from one plane of consciousness to another. This is the power and dominion implanted in man from the beginning. It is man's control over his thoughts and feelings. A quickening from on high must precede his realization of dominion. Power is increased through exalted ideas. The power of the voice controls all the vibratory energies of the organism. It is the open door between the formless and the formed worlds of vibrations pertaining to expression. Every word that goes forth receives its specific character from the power faculty.

Imagination   Every form and shape originated in the imagination. It
is through the imagination that the formless
takes form. Man is continually making and sending forth into his mind, his body, and the world
about him living thought forms embodied and
endued with his whole character. These images
are formed in the imaging faculty.

In the realm of the real, the imaging power
of the mind is innocent of error images. It is
open and receptive to the beauty and perfection
of Being. This faculty makes the great, when the
soul is lifted up with spiritual fervor. Exercised
without the Christ understanding, it is personal
credulity. It is not in itself error, but may be
used in erroneous ways. In the communication
of God with man this faculty plays an important
part.

Understanding   That in man which comprehends is understand-
ing. It comprehends and knows in wisdom. Its
comparisons are not made in the realm of form,
but in the realm of ideas. It knows how to accomplish things. Spiritual discernment reveals
that knowledge and intelligence are auxiliary
to understanding.

There are two ways of getting understanding. One is by following the guidance of Spirit

that dwells within, and the other is to go blindly ahead and learn through hard experience.

Intellectual understanding of Truth is a tremendous step in advance of sense consciousness, and its possession brings a temptation to use for selfish ends the wisdom and power thereby revealed.

Spiritual understanding is the quickening of the Spirit within. Spiritual understanding is the ability of the mind to apprehend and realize the laws of thought and the relation of ideas one to another.

Will   The will is the executive faculty of the mind and carries out the edicts of the I AM. All thoughts that go in and out of man's consciousness pass the gate at which sits the will. If the will understands its office, the character and value of every thought are inquired into and a certain tribute is exacted for the benefit of the whole man. When the will of man adheres to wisdom faithfully and carries out in its work the plans that are idealized in wisdom, it creates in man a consciousness of harmony and peace.

The will may be said to be the man, because it is the directive power that determines character formation. When man wills to do the will of God, he exercises his individual will in wisdom, love, and spiritual understanding. He builds spiritual character.

What man wills or decrees comes to pass in his experience. The will is the center in mind and body around which revolve all the activities that constitute consciousness. It is the avenue through which the I AM expresses its potentiality.

Order   The inner spirit of order is the spiritual way of life. The divine idea of order is the idea of adjustment. As this is established in man's thought, his mind and affairs will be at one with the universal harmony. The faculty of order in the mind holds every thought and act strictly to the Truth of Being, regardless of circumstances or environment. The development of man is under law. Man can never exercise dominion until he knows who and what he is and, knowing, brings forth that knowledge into the external by exercising it in divine order.

Zeal   Zeal is intensity, ardor, enthusiasm; the inward fire of the soul that urges man onward regardless of caution. It is the affirmative impulse of existence. Its command is "Go forward!" When zeal and judgment work together great things can be accomplished.

To be without zeal is to be without the zest of living. Zeal and enthusiasm incite to glorious achievement in every aim and ideal that the mind conceives. Energy is zeal in motion. Energy is the forerunner of every effect. Never repress the impulse, the force, the zeal welling up within you. Praise it for its great energy and efficiency in action.

Let your zeal be tempered with wisdom. Do not let your zeal run away with judgment. Man is a dynamo of pent-up power, but he needs judgment in its use. Always exercise zeal in spiritual ways. Extraordinary zeal in the accomplishment of some ideal develops what is called genius. Genius is the accumulated zeal of the individual in some chosen field of life action. Genius is the breaking forth of the accumulated achievements of a man in that field of activity for which he has been very zealous.

Renunciation   Renunciation is a letting go
                      of old thoughts in order
that new thoughts may find a place in consciousness. A healthy state of mind is attained when the thinker willingly lets go the old thoughts and takes on the new. This is illustrated by the inlet and outlet of a pool of water. Renunciation, sometimes called elimination, carries forward the work of elimination of error thoughts

from the mind and waste from the body.

It is just as necessary that one should learn to let go of thoughts, conditions, and substances in consciousness, body, and affairs, when they have served their purpose and one no longer needs them, as it is that one should lay hold of new ideas and new substances to meet one's daily requirements. Therefore it is very necessary that the eliminative faculty be quickened in one, and a right balance between receiving and giving, laying hold and letting go, be established.

Life In the phenomenal world, life is the energy that propels all forms of action. The life ego is the most subtle and most variable of all the powers of man. It presides over the life of the body. The pure life of God flows into man's consciousness through the spiritual body idea. Only those who have come into consciousness of the spiritual body idea can feel this holy stream of life. Its nature is to vivify with perpetual life all that it touches. It knows only to give, give unceasingly and eternally, without restraint. To desire to be instructed by God is the first step in exalting the inner life force. Life is divine, spiritual. Its source is Spirit. The river of life is within man in his spiritual consciousness. He comes into consciousness of the river of life through the quickening of Spirit. He can be truly quickened with new life and vitalized in mind and body only by consciously contacting Spirit.

Thinking

TO MAN is given the highest power in the universe, the conscious power of thought. There is a universal, creative force that urges man forward to the recognition of the creative power of his individual thought. This thought is elemental, and all its attributes come under the dominion of man. When he cooperates with Principle, man sits on the throne of his authority and the elemental force is subject to him.

Thinking is the formulating process of mind. The thinking faculty is the inlet and the outlet of all your ideas. It is active, zealous, impulsive, but not always wise. Its nature is to think, and think it will. The thinking faculty in you makes you a free agent, because it is your creative center. In and through this one power you establish your consciousness—you build your world.

Thought   Thought is a product of think-
                   ing. It is a mental vibration or impulse. Each thought is an identity that has a central ego around which all its elements revolve. Thoughts are capable of expressing themselves. Every thought clothes itself in a life form according to the character given it by the thinker. The form is simply the conclusion of the thought. The mind of man marshals its faculties and literally makes into living entities the thoughts that it entertains.

Energies (thought vibrations) are sent out by the force and power of thought. Thought power is the moving force within an idea that gives it expression. All structures are built by thought power. This power is transmitted from mind to mind and from mind to body in all living forms. The omnipresent, invisible substance (thought-stuff) is ever ready to take form in accordance with one's mental pattern. The thought-stuff of the universe is more sensitive than a phonograph record. It transcribes not only all sounds, but even the slightest vibration of thought.

Thought Aggregation

Like attracts like. A thought will take up its abode in our consciousness with thoughts of like character. This law of attraction continues until combined thoughts make a colony. This colony of thoughts expresses itself in the cells of the body—for good or ill. This collection or aggregation of ideas in the mind is a thought center. They build organs through which they manifest. The surrounding mental climate or thought atmosphere is created by each person in accordance with the character of his thinking. Thoughts of negation build a discordant atmosphere. Thoughts of love, prosperity, health, and faith create a harmonious mental atmosphere.

Thought Control

Thought is controlled by the right use of affirmation and denial—by the power of the mind to accept and reject. This power of the mind is the I AM, and it is through the avenue of I AM expression that thought control, dominion, and mastery are obtained. Thoughts are controlled by the mind through its power to say "yes" or "no." To "hold a thought" is to affirm or deny a certain proposition both mentally and audibly until the logic of the mind is satisfied and spiritual realization is attained.

Denial   Human consciousness is made up of a multitude of false personal and race beliefs. Denial is the mental process of erasing from consciousness the false beliefs. It clears away belief in evil as reality and thus makes room for the establishing of Truth. Through it we get rid of the shadows. We cleanse the mind. A denial is a relinquishment and should not be made with vehemence. Make denials as though you were gently sweeping away cobwebs.

Affirmation   When we poise ourselves in Divine Mind our denials and affirmations will be made in right relation. We will know just when to let go of a thought and when to lay hold of another.

The purpose of affirmation is to establish in consciousness a broad understanding of the divine principles on which all life and existence depend. By affirming Truth we are lifted out of false thinking into the consciousness of Spirit. An affirmation is a positive statement of Truth. By the use of it one claims and appropriates that which is his in Truth. It is the mental movement that asserts confidently and persistently the Truth of Being in the face of all appearances to the contrary. The sum total of thought in all its positive aspects composes the affirmations that bring ideas into form. They do not have to be made in set terms, words, or statements.

Affirmations of words of Truth realized in consciousness bring the mind into just the right attitude to receive light, power, and guidance from Spirit. Words are the vehicles through which ideas make themselves manifest. Words that have in them the realization of perfect, everywhere-present, always-present divine life, and our oneness with this life, are dominant in the restoration of life and health. When spiritual words abide in man's consciousness, the word or thought formed in the human mind must give way to the higher principles of Being.

The Decree   To decree is to command or to ordain. To decree with assurance is to establish and to fix an ideal in substance. The force behind the decree is invisible. It binds with invisible power the one who makes it. We have only a slight conception of the strength of the intangible. Affirmations are far stronger than the strongest visible thing in the world. Words charged with power and intelligence increase with use.

Thought and Word   Man cannot know
                            how the thought or
word work except through his own consciousness. He must understand, control, and put in
order his own thought and word. Our most important study is our own consciousness. By a
right understanding, and by using right thoughts
and words, man will experience the kingdom
within him.

Thoughts are capable of expressing themselves. They think. Man thinks. He thinks into
his thoughts all that he is. There is a difference
between the original thinking and the secondary
thought. One has its animating center in Spirit;
the other, in thought. One is Son of God; the
other is son of man. If man conformed to the
divine creative law, his word would make things
instantly.

Every word has its effect, though unseen and
unrecognized. What we think, we usually express in words. Our words bring about in our
life and affairs whatever we put into them. A
weak thought is followed by words of weakness.
Through the law of expression and form, words
of weakness change to weakness the character
of everything that receives them.

Talk about nervousness and weakness produces corresponding conditions. Sending forth
the word of strength and affirming poise will

bring about the desired strength and poise. Every time we speak we cause the atoms of the body to tremble and change their places. Not only do we cause the atoms of our own body to change their position, but we raise or lower the rate of vibration and otherwise affect the bodies of others with whom we come in contact. Thus, every word brings forth after its kind.

Directive Word Power   The spoken word carries vibrations through the universe and moves the intelligence inherent in every form, animate or inanimate. Man, the highest emanation of Divine Mind, has great directive power and is really co-operator with God in forming the universe. We should be speaking words of Truth to everything. There are no secrets and no concealments.

The power of the word is given man to use. The better he understands the character of God and his own relation to humanity, the more unselfishly will he exercise this power. Some are using this power in selfish ways. This should not deter others who have a better understanding of the law from using it in right ways. When we need things necessary to our happiness, it is not sacrilegious to set in action this higher law in attaining them. The word of one in authority carries weight and produces far-reaching effects.

If your word is selfish, that which will come
to you through its use will be unsatisfactory.
Learn to speak right words only. It is your duty
as expresser of the divine law to speak forth
the Logos, the very Word of God, to manifest
for you and in you its innate perfection.

Thought and Act   Every act of man has
                           its origin in thought,
which is expressed into the phenomenal world
from a mental center that is but a point of radiation for an energy that lies back of it. That
point of radiation is the conscious I, which in
its correct relation is one with Cause, and has
at its command all the power potential in Cause.

The conscious I can look in two directions—
to the outer world where the thoughts that rise
within it give sensation and feeling, which ultimate in a moving panorama of visibility; or to
the world within, whence all its life, power,
and intelligence are derived. When the I looks
wholly within, it loses all sense of the external.
When it looks wholly without, upon sensation
and feeling, it loses its bearings in the maze of
its own thought creations. Then it builds up a
belief of separateness from, and independence
of, a causing power. Man sees only form and
makes his God a personal being located in a
city of dimensions. This belief of separateness

leads to ignorance. When the soul thinks itself something alone, it cuts itself off in consciousness from the fount of inspiration. Believing himself separate from his source, man loses sight of the divine harmony. The only walls of separation are those built by consciousness of separation.

Thought Forms Many factors enter into the process of thinking. The capacity of the thinker to form thoughts, to give them substance and force, is the great factor. The understanding of right and wrong, truth and error, substance and shadow, is important. Many significant conditions enter into that mental process loosely termed thinking.

Every mental process is generative. From thinking is evolved what is called living. Thinking is formative. Thought clothes itself in a life form according to the character given it by the thinker. Every thought produces a living organism. Thought is creative and covers every phase of life. Every life expression originated in some thought. All of the detestable thoughts that mankind harbors, produce living organisms after their kind.

Error Thoughts Error thoughts represent belief in thoughts and beliefs not of God. They are untrue. They have no foundation in Truth. Error thought is a product of the fallen human consciousness. It is negation or evil. Evil is a parasite. It has no permanent life of itself. Its whole existence depends on the life it borrows from its parent. When its connection with the parent is severed, nothing remains. In Divine Mind there are no evil conditions. Such conditions have no basis of reality. They are conjurations of a false consciousness. Apparent evil is the result of ignorance. When Truth is presented, the error disappears.

Man has the privilege and freedom of using God-power as he will. When he misuses it he brings about inharmonious conditions. These are called evil. Evil appears in the world because man is not in spiritual understanding. He can do away with evil by learning rightly to use the one Power. If there were a power of evil, it could not be changed.

Experimentation   Man is a free agent. He can open his mind to divine wisdom and know creative law, or he can work out his unfoldment through experimentation. Our human race is in the experimental stage. In our ignorance we transgress the law to the very limit, and then a great reaction sets in, a general condition that is negative to the point of dissolution. Then that in us which always looks obediently to God in an extremity is awakened, and we seek divine guidance. The human race has formed laws of physical birth and death, laws of sickness and inability, laws that recognize no other source of existence except the physical. The sum total of these laws forms a race consciousness separate from and independent of creative Mind. When creative Mind seeks to help men spiritually, the human mind opposes it and makes every effort to solve its problems in its own way.

The great need of the human family is mind control. Mastery is attained through realization of the power of Spirit.

The Spoken Word

IN PURE metaphysics there is but one word, the Word of God. This is the original creative Word, or thought, of Being. In the original it includes wisdom, judgment, power, and all the inherent potentialities of Being.

Divine Mind creates under law; that is, mental law. First is mind, then the idea in mind of what the act shall be, then the act itself. In Divine Mind the idea is referred to as the Word.

Man is the consummation of the Word. The perfect Word of God is Spiritual Man. It is through Spiritual Man that all things are made. There is but one idea of man in Divine Mind. That idea is the perfect pattern of man's character.

As an imitator of Divine Mind, man has power to form and make manifest whatsoever he idealizes. Unless his thoughts are unified with Divine Mind and guided in their operations by infinite wisdom, his thought forms are perishable.

Surroundings and Thought Vibrations

The self of man is spiritual. When it is in direct conscious unity with the Father-Mind it has permanent formative power. Even in his ignorant use of thought, man's mind is forming conditions, even to the changing of the face of nature itself. Every thought that goes forth from the brain sends vibrations into the surrounding atmosphere and moves the realm of things to action. The effect is in proportion to the ability of the thinker to concentrate his mental forces.

The average thought vibration produces but temporary results. Under intense mind activity, conditions more or less permanent are impressed upon the sensitive plate of the universal. Through this activity they are brought into physical manifestation.

Spoken Word   Every idea originating in Divine Mind is expressed in the mind of man. Through the thought of man the Divine Mind idea is brought to the outer plane of consciousness. Through movement on what is termed the conscious, or most outer, plane of action, the thought takes expression as the spoken word. There is in the formed conscious man, or body, a point of concentration for this word. Through this point the word is expressed in invisible vibrations.

Following the creative law in its operation from the formless to the formed, we can see how an idea fundamental in Divine is grasped by the man ego, how it takes form in his thought, and how it is later expressed through the spoken word. If man conformed to the divine law, his word would make things instantly. He has lost, in a measure, knowledge of the steps in the creative process from the within to the without.

The mental emanation and the creative word are the forces that stimulate the receptive intelligence of nature. When we believe what we hear, there is formed in us the substance of the word.

Words and Zeal   Words of Truth from a
zealous man possess dynamic power to heal and bless because the spiritual man enters into them. This is why they move multitudes and are not stayed by conditions of time. When the zone of Spirit, from which healing words emanate, is unobstructed, they feed the souls of men and are creative as well as re-creative.

This is why the sayings of the prophets and mystics have such enduring qualities. They are attached by invisible currents of life to the one Great Spirit. They have within them the germ of perfect wholeness that keeps them perpetually increasing.

The true prophet of God does not even have to write his words down. He may speak them and through their own inherent power of perpetuation and growth they will find their way into the minds of men to uplift and heal. Jesus did not write a line except in the sand, yet His words are treasured today as the most precious that we have.

Living Words   The word of Truth has life
in it. It has power to restore and make whole. It cannot perish or grow less with the changes that come with the fleeting years. The more spiritual the individual is who

gives forth the words the more enduring they are, and the more powerfully the words move men the more surely they awaken them to their divine nature.

The words of Jesus were given to common people—according to the world's standard—by a carpenter in a remote corner of the earth. Yet these words have moved men for more than nineteen hundred years to realize, to dare, and to do as no other words that were ever uttered.

The Inner Word   Jesus spoke in terms of that inner Word which creates all things. He knew that His words were vivified with a life essence and a moving power that would demonstrate the truth of His statement.

These words have rung through the souls of men and set them afire with God's Spirit throughout the ages. This is because they are spiritual words, words that have within them the seeds of a divine life, of a perfect wholeness. They grow in the minds of all who give them place.

Spiritual Law

ALL SANE persons acknowledge the necessity of observing law in their daily living. The great majority have a human standard. Now the whole race is awakening to the knowledge of a higher source of existence. More people every day are giving attention to the law of Spirit in their life.

We find in the Scriptures constant reference, in symbols and also in direct language, to order as a fundamental law of the universe and of man. All peoples have observed this, and especially the people of God. Paul said, "All things should be done decently and in order."

Remedy   Suggestion is systematically used in the business world, and unless you are strong in your own convictions as to what your needs are, you will be loaded up with many things for which you have no use. The remedy is to establish yourself in the spiritual law. You will come under one or the other of these laws, the manmade or the spiritual, and it is for you to choose which is best.

Whatever there is in mind, body, or affairs that is out of harmony is easily adjusted when you open the way in your mind for the manifestation of divine order.

Jesus' Birth   The birth of Jesus was foretold and arranged beforehand. It was not left to chance. His mother "magnified" the Lord before He was born. This illustrates the truth that it is necessary to have order from the very beginning. The bringing forth of John the Baptist is an example of the coming of another state of consciousness and of the necessity of law and order in prenatal culture.

The same law holds good in our body and our affairs. The power of the word should be expressed in our homes. We should surround ourselves with words suggestive of spiritual things. If words count, and we know they do, we should be careful of every belief taken into consciousness through the eye as well as through the ear.

Suggestion From their inception to their expression, words are important. The law is fulfilled not only in mind but in manifestation also. Every suggestion that enters the mind brings forth like expression in act. The time is coming when it will be unlawful to print in the daily papers any record of crime or of anything that will bring discord into the minds of readers.

Once I read of a man who committed a crime, and in his pocket was found a newspaper clipping describing almost identically the same criminal act. His crime was the fruit of suggestion. How many such suggestions does one large daily paper carry to its thousands of readers in its recital of the daily horrors that make up the news?

As the world comes more and more under the spiritual law editors and publishers will not ask their readers what they want, but will give them what they should have for mental food. And as the people are raised to higher

planes of consciousness they will demand reading of an uplifting character. They will be just
as careful as regards what they read as they are
now beginning to be in reference to food. There
will be the same demand for pure reading as
for pure food. If it is against the law of the land
to adulterate food, how much more is it against
the law of right thinking to adulterate the truth!
We can see the necessity of order and law according to Spirit. If we would demonstrate
health, every deleterious thought should be kept
out of our mental atmosphere even more carefully than harmful elements are kept out of our
material food.

Food and Clothing   This spiritual law is
                           operative in food
and clothing. If we think about order and harmony our taste in material things will change.
We shall desire the purest foods, and there will
be more harmony in the colors we choose to
wear. Man stands above all creation. He has
power to clothe himself in the richness and glory
of Spirit. Out of the air we may manufacture
the things we eat and wear. This is not a flight
of fancy. It is not an assumption of theoretical
metaphysics that we may be able to make our
food and clothing from the air, but a logical
conclusion that follows the understanding of

God as the omnipresent source of all that appears.

If you are disorderly and indefinite along any line, put yourself at once under the order of Divine Mind by affirming daily that the same law that swings the stars is operative in and through your life and your affairs.

One Law   All people who have studied metaphysics and understand somewhat the action of the mind recognize that there is one underlying law and that through this law all things come into expression; also that there is one universal Mind, the source and sole origin of all real intelligence. First is mind, then mind expresses itself in ideas, then the ideas make themselves manifest. This is a metaphysical statement of the divine Trinity, Father, Son, and Holy Spirit. The trinity Mind, the expression of Mind, and the manifestations of Mind are found in simple numbers and complex combinations everywhere.

I Am   In the King James Bible the Hebrew "Jehovah" has been translated "Lord." *Lord* means an external ruler. Bible students say that *Jehovah* means the self-existent One, the I AM. Then instead of reading "Lord" we should read "I AM." It makes a great difference whether we think of I AM, self-existence within, or "Lord," master without.

All Scripture shows that *Jehovah* means just what God told Moses it meant: I AM. So instead of "Lord" say "I AM" whenever you read it and you will get a clearer understanding and realization of what Jehovah is.,

God was known to the Israelites as Jehovah-shalom: "I am peace." You can demonstrate peace of mind by holding the words *"I am peace."*

If we start any such demonstration and try to apply the I AM to personality, we fall short. This is frequently the cause of lack of results in carrying out the laws that all metaphysicians recognize as fundamentally true.

The mind does not always comprehend the I AM in its highest, neither does it discern that the all-knowing, omnipotent One is within man. This recognition must be cultivated, and everyone should become conscious of the I AM presence. This consciousness will come through prayer and meditation upon Truth. In Truth there is but one I AM, Jehovah, the omnipotent I AM that is eternally whole and perfect.

If you take Jehovah-shalom into your mind and hold it with the thought of a mighty peace, you will feel a consciousness, a harmonizing stillness, that no man can understand. This consciousness is healing in itself. It must be felt, realized, and acknowledged by your individual I AM before the supreme I AM can pour out its power. Then you will know that you have touched something; but you cannot explain to another just what it is, because you have gone beyond the realm of words and made union with the divine cause. It is the quickening of your divinity through the power of the word. This divine nature is in us all, waiting to be brought into expression through our recognition of the power and might of the I AM; to Jehovah-rapha, which is "I am he that healeth thee."

Inner and Outer   We should not fail to think always of the spiritual law under which the I AM moves. It is possible for man to take I AM power and apply it in external ways and leave out the true spiritual law. We are proclaiming that man can use I AM power to restore health and bring increased happiness; in fact, that through righteous, lawful use of the I AM he can have everything that he desires. But some people are using this power in a material way, neglecting soul culture, building up the external without taking the intermediate step between the supreme Mind and its manifestation in the outer.

We should remember that the soul must

grow as well as the body. For example, a man was overtaken with physical disability and loss of eyesight some years ago. In his extremity he turned to the spiritual law for help and was very faithful in its mental application. Time passed before I saw him again; his physical condition was unchanged, but there was a great change in his mind. He had found the light and he was filled with inward rejoicing. He had become blind that he might see. However his family thought all his dependence upon Truth had been a failure because his physical sight had not been restored. During all these years he managed his business, and it prospered, and his family was well provided for. He was himself for a time disappointed and rebellious because his eyes were not healed. Then he became glad, because through the prayers and meditations he found the inner light. His physical sight will be restored when he has made the complete connection between mind and body.

If you find yourself disappointed because you do not at once demonstrate health or success, be at peace and know that your earnest prayers and meditations are working out in you a soul growth that will yet become manifest beyond your greatest hopes.

It is easier to seek the Truth willingly and be watchful and obedient than it is to be forced by some severe experience. Hard experiences are not necessary if we are obedient to the Truth that saves us from them. Time should be given to prayer and meditation daily. We cannot grow without them, and no man who neglects them will successfully develop his spiritual powers.

Unification Before you can realize the mighty power of ideas you must unify them. All must pull together. Get your ideas in divine order, and a mighty mind force will begin to work for you right away. This divine order is necessary to the upbuilding of both mind and body. This divine order is the "kingdom of heaven" so often referred to by Jesus. To attain this unity and harmony of mind it is necessary to have perfect statements of Truth and to adhere to them in thought and word.

Ideas change the race thought atmosphere. Jesus had a grasp of divine ideas. If we believe in and follow Him we shall come into the Christ state of mind. We become like-minded by entering into the absolute Mind. In the absolute Mind there is only harmony.

As man unifies his own mind forces in the one Mind his body is lifted up into a new state of harmony. If he is not demonstrating this principle, it is because he is not unified with the

one great harmonious Mind. He is not expressing this Mind as he should because he is not
realizing his oneness with it.

Resolve to become one with God through
Christ. Harmonize yourself with Him and all
your world will be in harmony. Be on the alert
to see harmony everywhere. Do not magnify
seeming differences. Do not keep up any petty
divisions but continually declare the one universal harmony. This will insure perfect order
and wholeness. The Christ Mind is here as the
unifying principle of this race. We must believe
in this mind working in us and through us and
know that through it we are joined to the
Father-Mind. In the consciousness of the Father-
Mind the unity of God and man is demonstrated.

Prayer

IT IS unthinkable that the Creator should cause to exist a creation so inferior to Himself as to remove it beyond the pale of fellowship with Him. In his wise moments man knows that this is not logical or true. It is man's exalted concepts of God and his disparaging beliefs about himself that have built the mental wall that separates them.

Thus man must understand the nature of

God and awaken in himself that divine nature through which to effect his conscious union with Him. God is Spirit. We are the offspring of this Spirit. God is Mind: man is the thinker. God is Life: man is the living. God is Substance: man is form and shape. God is Power: man is powerful. God is Wisdom: man is wise. God is Love: man is loving. God is Truth: man is truthful.

God-Mind is a treasure field of all potentialities within man in which is found the fulfillment of every need one can possibly have. What we need to know above all is that there is this place within our soul where we can consciously meet God and receive a flood of new life into not only our mind but also our body. With a right understanding of man's relation to his potentialities his soul grows with infinite capacity.

Intimate Spirit   The intimate connecting spirit that unites man and his source is the divine Logos. It is in the highest sense an innate spiritual umbilical cord that connects us with the Holy Mother from whom we can receive a perpetual flow of life. Because of this man instinctively feels and knows from whence his help comes. In the divine Logos is the living impetus that vitalizes the soul of man and enables him to develop his latent powers.

Soul Urge The highest avenue through which God can express Himself is man. All growth and unfoldment from atom to sun is based upon the law of soul urge. The hungering for God that is felt by man in his soul is really God hungering to express through man. The Spirit of God in man is constantly working, yes, steadily and persistently working, to transmute every natural impulse of mind and soul into a spiritual realization of life. God is always seeking to awaken man's whole soul to His mighty presence. He is working to satisfy man's inner craving with living substance and intelligence, thus expanding and rounding his soul and body consciousness, offering him opportunity to express Divine Mind itself more fully and more perfectly.

Desire Deep desire is essential for spiritual growth. It is the onward impulse of the ever-evolving soul. It builds from within outward and carries its fulfillment with it as a necessary corollary. Man has never had a desire that could not somewhere, in the providence of God, be fulfilled. If this were not true, the universe would be weak at its most vital point.

Sincere desire is a form of prayer. Every impulse or desire of the soul for life, love, light, is a prayer. It is a conscious expression of an upward trend of nature found everywhere. Earnest, intense desire draws the whole being up out of mortality and its transient joys into the power to appreciate and receive real spiritual blessings.

Prayer without desire in it, prayer without sincerity in it, prayer without soul in it, prayer without Spirit in it is fruitless prayer. So, when you frame your desires in sound words and place them before your indwelling Lord, you are using intelligently the supreme law of God in bringing into manifestation that which He has implanted in you.

Spiritual Character   We find prayer to be many-sided; it is not only asking but receiving, also. We must pray believing that we shall receive. Prayer is both invocation and affirmation. Meditation, concentration, denial, and affirmation in the silence are all forms of what is loosely termed prayer.

Through prayer we develop the highest phase of character. Spiritual character building is from within outward. Spiritual character lives in man. It is what God has engraved on man's soul, ready for development through man's spiritual efforts. It is a reserve force of organized victory over human thought.

Man builds spiritual character by consciously functioning in God-Mind where, laying hold of spiritual ideas, he realizes the Truth they contain. He thus weaves them into his soul consciousness and they become a part of his very nature.

Conscious Union   All down the ages man has been making the spiritual effort to realize conscious union with that innermost center where Truth in all its glory abides eternally. Actually, prayer is man's steady effort to know God. He can make conscious contact with Spirit by turning his attention away from material things and thinking about Spirit. Through prayer he gains an intimate relationship with God.

The ability to merge our mind into the one Mind makes a great man of us. When man awakens even a slight consciousness of the cooperative Spirit, he becomes a co-creator with God. There is a partial conscious unity with Spirit and there is a complete conscious unity with Spirit; however, whenever man wholly merges his mind with the creative Mind he is in the consciousness in which his prayers are fulfilled. He finds that he can adjust any condition that comes into his life.

Everyone should pray. Prayer does not change God! It changes us!

Effective prayer does not agonize. No man

who has fused his soul with the soul of God has suffered or agonized. The suffering comes as a result of separation and the effort to return to the consciousness of Omnipresence.

Accept the urge to begin the practice of prayer. Through it make contact with the Source of your being. In prayer you are able to recognize the Source. As you practice prayer your innate Spirit showers its life energies into your conscious mind and a great soul expansion follows.

In your prayers you must meet God face to face and realize that you are getting that inner assurance which is the real answer. Your most effective prayers are those in which you rise above all consciousness of time and space. In this state of mind you automatically contact the Spirit of God. When you elevate your consciousness to Spirit, the God presence becomes meaningful to you. The God presence is an abiding flame, a flame of life, of life everlasting in every cell and fiber of being making you more alive, cleansing and purifying until you become every whit perfect. During high realizations of Truth you are conscious of this abiding flame that works in and through you.

In this state of at-one-ment you truly become aware of sublimity and power. The God presence establishes you in spiritual ideas which are needed factors in the unfoldment of the whole man.

Interest   In prayer what should be our attitude, our interest, as we approach the divine presence? If we knew that right now we were about to be ushered into the presence of Jesus, to what extent would our spiritual expectancy be aroused? No doubt we should be thrilled through and through at the mere thought. Let us feel this same intense interest, this same concern, as we approach the divine presence within ourself. It will add much to the readiness with which we receive Truth.

Asking   Understanding shows that prayer is more than asking God for help in this physical world. Actually, we have become a human race of praying beggars. Prayer is not supplication or begging. It is more than supplication. Supplication is impotent. Do not supplicate or beg God to give you what you need. Prayer is a simple asking for that which we know is waiting for us at the hands of our Father and an affirmation of its existence.

When Jesus advised asking for what we want, He was instructing us to be persistent in our demands. People ignorant of the relation in which man stands to God wonder why we

should ask and even importune a Father who
has provided all things for us. This is explained
when we perceive that God is a great mind reservoir that has to be tapped by man's mind and
poured into visibility through his thought and
word. If the mind of man is clogged with doubt,
lethargy, or fear, he must open the way by persistent knocking and asking. Acquire in prayer
a facility in asking equal to the mathematician's
expertness in handling numbers and you will
get responses in proportion.

Undoubtedly the one thing that stands out
prominently in the teaching of Jesus is the
necessity of prayer. He prayed on the slightest
pretext, or in some such manner invoked the
presence of God. He prayed over situations that
most men would deal with without the inter-
vention of God. If He were verily God incarnate, the skeptic often asks, why did He so
often appeal to an apparently higher God? To
answer this doubt intelligently and truly one
must understand the constitution of man.

There are always two men in each individual.
The man without is the picture that the man
within paints with his mind. This mind is the
open door to the unlimited principle of Being.
When Jesus prayed He was setting into action
the various powers of His individuality in order
to bring about certain results. Within His iden-

tity was of God; without He was human personality.

Prayer with a Purpose

When we pray, let us pray with a purpose. Purpose gives life a real meaning. Purpose gives joy and zest to living. When our eye is on the goal we are not so easily perturbed. Purpose awakens new trains of thought. Purpose directs these trains of thought into new fields of achievement. To succeed we must have some great purpose in mind, some goal toward which we are to work. Above all, we must always purpose in our heart to achieve spiritually. As we study the one great Presence and Power, we come to know that there is no chapter in our life that is such a failure but has back of it a grand purpose, which purpose must eventually somewhere, somehow work itself out in a most ennobling manner.

Communion with God

Prayer is communion between God and man. This communion takes place in the innermost part of man's being. It is the only way to cleanse and perfect the consciousness.

Prayer is the most highly accelerated mind action known. It steps up mental action until man's consciousness synchronizes with the Christ

Mind. It is the language of spirituality. When developed, prayer makes man master in the realm of creative ideas.

As in all matters where we seek divine help we are free to use any words we choose or no words at all. However, to a person in the understanding of Truth, prayer should be an affirmation of that which is in Being. What is the necessity of the prayer of affirmation if Being already is? In order that the creative law of the Word may be fulfilled. What you earnestly desire and persistently affirm will be yours.

The Silence   The highest form of prayer
                       we know is quietly entering
the inner chamber within the soul, shutting the door to the external thoughts of daily life, and seeking conscious union with God. Prayer is man's steady effort to know God. Through prayer we gain an intimate relationship with God. The purpose of the silence is to still the activity of the personal thought so that the still small voice of God may be heard. For in the silence Spirit speaks Truth to us and just that Truth of which we stand in need.

When entering the silence, close the eyes and ears to the without. Go to God within and hold the mind steadily on the word until that word illumines the whole inner consciousness.

Think what the mighty vitalizing energy of God releases. Penetrate deep into God consciousness within yourself and hold your prayer word steadily until you attain spiritual realization and the logic of your own mind is satisfied.

To realize an idea in the silence is to clothe it with life, substance, and intelligence. To realize a prayer is to actualize it. To realize it is to clothe it with soul, to know there is fulfillment.

The word of prayer has in it a living seed that is bound to impregnate the soil of the mind and cause it to bring forth fruit after its kind.

Intellectual and Spiritual Silence It is man's concept of God that makes prayer intellectual or spiritual. There is a vast difference between mere intellectual silence and that constructive silence which always gives the victory within the soul. The intellectual silence, which is limited in power, is the silence where one's whole attention is fixed on the intellect. The intellect has thought its power supreme. While it is a wonderful faculty, it is in truth the tool of Spirit. As such it needs discipline if it is to be able to perform its perfect work. The intellect is always busy, jumping from one thing to another. Much of the time it dwells on the daily routine of the

workaday world or on conditions in the world
at large. The first step in scientific silence is
simply to still these outer intellectual thoughts
so that the consciousness may become subser-
vient to the Spirit within.

The operation of prayer saves the soul from
all past and future mistakes. In prayer we are
led not to doubt, distrust, or hate man but to
love him with all our mind, soul, and strength.
Instead of fighting life and struggling to com-
pete with millions of others in the same foolish
war, we cooperate. Instead of wasting energy in
tearing down, we conserve in building up.
Prayer shows humanity how to love life, how to
love the Author of life, and how to love life's
activities. In this state of consciousness man
automatically drops the burdens of the intellect
and enters into the freedom of real living. Man
must have the spiritual ability to discern life's
perfect pattern if he is to fulfill the requirements
of scientific prayer.

By quieting the mental man, by passing
through the discipline of intellectual silence,
man arrives at the very threshold of God's work-
shop, the threshold of Being. As he passes into
the inner chamber he finds he is entering the
holy of holies, where noiselessly, silently, a
mighty work is always going on. God works in
the stillness.

As man comes into the presence of God with his prayer in the form of an affirmation of Truth, holding the prayer steadily in mind and consciously unifying his mind with the mind of God, he is aware only of the soundlessness of God's Word as it weaves itself in and out through the whole soul and body consciousness, illumining, redeeming, and restoring him according to his faith and trust, according to his strength and power to receive.

Meditation   Persistent meditation on the Truth contained in the Word of God opens the mind to a greater inflow of Spirit. When we let our meditations fall on the knowing part of ourself, we go into a higher mental state or an exalted condition of mind, wherein we receive a higher and clearer conception of things spiritual. Every student of Truth builds the Christ body as he constantly abides in the Christ mind through daily meditation upon words of Truth. Then all words become quickening life and nourishing substance in both mind and body.

Attention and Concentration   In prayer attention is the concentration of the mind upon a statement of Truth. Man can take a word of Truth and through "one-pointed" mind concentration unite his consciousness with the Mind of God. He can hold a realizing prayer until the truth it contains is engrafted into the very soul. Through the engrafted word, he becomes a strong, positive spiritual character.

Attention is focalizing the I AM or inner entity upon a word of prayer, until the inner meaning is realized and the soul is aware of a definite spiritual uplift. As a lens focalizes the sun's rays at a given point—and we know how intense that point of light may become—concentration focalizes the mind on a single idea until it becomes manifest and objective.

In concentration the Holy Spirit works through the divine mother substance to bring forth the fruits of Divine Mind. The Holy Spirit is the teacher. The teacher and the student use the same principles, but the teacher arouses and inspires the student to greater achievement. The Holy Spirit urges us to great spiritual effort.

When we direct the mental powers upon a definite idea, faith plays its part. It is involved in concentration. As we give attention to the idea through one-pointed mind concentration, we break into a realm of finer mind activity.

Realization   In spiritual silence man's realization is established in his heart and he has the assurance that his prayer is answered and that the law of demonstration brings forth the fruit. The realization is written not only in the soul but in the intellect. The intellect always perceives what has taken place within and has power to retain its perception and to express itself accordingly. Thus the intellect serves Spirit, and as it unfolds it becomes more and more like Spirit. It becomes in deed and in truth the instrument of God.

Realization is the deep inner conviction and assurance of the fulfillment of an ideal. It means at-one-ment, completion, perfection, wholeness, repose, resting in God. It is the dawning of Truth in the consciousness. When realization takes place, one abides in the light of God-Mind. It is the inner conviction that prayer has been answered, although there is as yet no outer manifestation.

The supreme realization is unity with God-Mind.

Constructive thought force is a great and mighty power. When it is realized in the silence it becomes the one and only power in all the earth. The understanding of this makes one an adept in the domain of scientific prayer.

Prayer and Faith   It is necessary to pray believing that we have received because God is all that we desire. The good always exists in Divine Mind as ideas. We bring it into manifestation through the prayer of faith, affirmation, praise, and acknowledgment.

Within the deep stillness of the soul, listen first to the innate voice of faith. Man builds up an enduring state of faith by repeated realizations of Truth. The illumination thus gained comes forth in man as spiritual understanding expressed in sound words. Faith draws upon substance. Dynamic, creative, transforming power is roused to spiritual action when man affirms his unity with Almightiness and his undaunted faith in its power.

Man must not only be submissive and obedient to the divine law, but he must also realize that he is the offspring of the Ruler of the universe. When asking the Father for that which belongs to the Son under the divine law, man should assume the power and dignity of the Prince of Peace. He should not crawl and cringe before an imaginary king on a throne. Instead he should feel that he is the image of an invisible Being who has created him to represent His mightiness as well as His lovingkindness.

The prayer of faith is not supplication, a begging God to give things to man. Prayer at its highest is the entry through faith into a realm of mind forces that when rightly contacted change the character of every cell in brain and body.

Faith, the conviction of a higher providing Source, is based upon spiritual logic or innate reason and on the certainty that an all-wise and all-powerful Creator's plan includes necessary provision for His offspring. When man emerges from the limitations of human consciousness and feels within him the stirring of Spirit, he finds that it is supremely logical and true that Spirit has provided for his supply and support.

When we have achieved spiritual realization of our prayer and our innermost soul is satisfied, we have the assurance that the thing is accomplished in Spirit and must become manifest. We may continue in our realization of faith until the whole consciousness responds and the instantaneous demonstration takes place. Prayer is impotent and unfruitful when the one who prays is without the firm belief that his prayers are answered. When man turns wholeheartedly to God, the prayer of faith brings forth abundantly. Since the prayer of faith is the activity of divine love, let us pray without ceasing, knowing that God hears and grants our petitions.

Faith is the fire of Spirit. Faith opens the door into an inner consciousness, where we hold the word steadily in mind until the spiritual substance responds to our word. Earnest, steady, and continued attention along this line is bound to bring forth the fruits of the Spirit in abundant measure. A steady, unwavering devotion of heart to the Spirit develops in us supermind qualities.

Prayer and Praise   Praise is the quality of
                                        mind that eulogizes
the good. It is one of the avenues through which spirituality expresses. The purpose of praise is to awaken in ourself a higher realization of the omnipresence and power of God. Prayer and praise change man, not God. The mental attitude that praise sets up stimulates, quickens, whirls into action, and finally establishes in character the ideals of which it is the vehicle. Through an inherent law of mind action we increase whatever we praise. Make practical application of the law of praise by giving thanks always for all things.

Prayer and Joy   No man yet knows all of
                                     life's joys, nor will he un-
til he has come into the full understanding of spiritual communion with God. No man knows the fullness of life, nor its joys, until he has prayed in meekness and thanksgiving and has received the sweet, pure realizations of Spirit.

True and lasting joy arises from within. The nature of the deep inner life is revealed only to those who spiritually penetrate into its source.

If you would feed the soul on the joys of Spirit, you must realize them and give thanks in prayer for the more abundant life. Then you find that a great subconscious well of living water will begin to bubble up in your soul. You will come to know that hitherto you have been living in the shallows of life instead of in its mighty depths. You will be blessed with a knowledge of the unity of all things, and a great peace and harmony will well up within.

It is impossible to found a lasting stronghold within on anything less than the understanding that God is a God of joy. It is through our realization of this truth that we drink heartily of the wine of life. Often even during serene, yes, sober moments, the inner man is athrill with some newborn, joyful anticipation. In prayer every high realization that comes to us is to strengthen us for greater achievements.

Conditions for True Prayer   These are the seven necessary conditions for true prayer: 1. God should be recognized as Father. 2. Oneness with God should be acknowledged. 3. Prayer must be made within, in "the secret place." 4. The door must be closed on all thoughts and interests of the outer world. 5. The one who prays must believe that he has received. 6. The kingdom of God must be desired above all things, and sought first. 7. The mind must let go of every unforgiving thought.

Truth Demonstrates Itself

TRUTH must be demonstrated. It defines itself. Truth is that which is true in the pure logic of the mind, regardless of appearances. We can talk about Truth. We can write books describing Truth, but we must realize the informing intelligence of the Spirit of truth. Truth is a quickening, creative energy. Truth is established by Divine Mind omnipresent, and the Spirit of truth is now right here.

We enter into the consciousness of the Spirit of truth by recognizing that it is. We enter into Spirit by praying and affirming.

Truth demonstrates all its propositions. Jesus represented Truth. He was Truth. He had but to call attention to His works to prove His authority. Jesus delegated all authority for His doctrine to the Spirit of truth.

The Truth, as demonstrated by Jesus Christ, is a restorative power. It restores all things to their divine order. Error has torn down the natural world, including man. Man is God manifest. If he is not demonstrating the perfect structure of divine life, there is ruin somewhere. Jesus demonstrated that Truth proves itself in restoring perfect order and wholeness.

Know the Truth   When you "know the truth" in substance, in life, in power, in love, in all its qualities, your body will demonstrate it. Your eyes will receive their sight, and your ears will be opened; you will walk as you never walked before; and that poor, sinking, empty spirit in you will have the "good tidings" preached to it.

Jesus did not mean that people poor in worldly things would have the gospel preached to them, and that rich people would go without it. He meant that those who were poor in spiritual things would, because of their open mind, eagerly receive the words of Truth.

Truth does not demonstrate its abiding

power until it is understood. That is why the people whom Jesus raised from the dead died again—they did not get the quickened understanding of Truth. Propositions of Truth must be thought out and lived out to be fully demonstrated. Many people are deluded by cramming the intellect with lessons on Truth. One Truth statement understood and demonstrated in life is worth more than many lessons and statements about Truth. Every mental process involves brain action, and spiritual knowledge demands the deepest kind of thought.

Something Intuitive   There is an intuitive something in us that tells us, when we think, when we meditate, what Truth is. For God reveals Himself to every one of us when we, with open mind, listen—listen to the word of Being itself. "It is the spirit in a man, the breath of the Almighty, that makes him understand."

You can analyze God. You have a right to. Men have been taught that they are poor, weak, and ignorant, that the finite cannot comprehend the infinite. Inner logic and the Spirit of truth assure that there is neither great nor small in Divine Mind.

Man is the offspring of the one omnipresent Mind. He has the capacity in him to know that

Mind. He has the power to know himself as the one Divine Mind manifest. Consequently all men can know and comprehend God. Divine Mind is open to us through the Spirit of truth. This understanding clears away all the fogs of personality, ignorance, and superstition; all the wrong beliefs that we have had about the character of God and man. When with your I AM you pierce these limited concepts of yourself and God that have separated you from your real being, the Spirit of truth will open your higher understanding.

Toward Perfection   We know that the tendency of the universe is toward perfection. Everything is striving to perfect itself. Where does the initial force come from? We say that it comes from nature; and nature is another name for God. Divine perfection is making happy and joyous everything and everybody in the universe. This is good; so we intuitively and logically listen to our higher reason, and arrive at the conclusion that God is good. This is the first postulate and conclusion of Truth: God is good and good is all.

Can you stick to that proposition in spite of all appearances? If you can, the Spirit of truth is working within you. But you have something to do to maintain your position. You will find, when you declare this word of Truth, that there will crowd into your mind every appearance of evil, and the voices, outer and inner, will say to you: "Oh, yes, of course, God in essence, in Spirit, away off somewhere in heaven, is good; but here is a world of evil. See the evil in the world; see the evil in man; behold the evil tendencies in yourself!" But in the face of all error you must demonstrate: "God is good and good is all."

God Is All-Powerful

Then you must lay hold of another quality of the infinite good: "God is all-powerful." Now, remember that Divine Mind is made up of ideas. Each one of these ideas must be wheeled into line in man's mind before he can put on the fullness of Truth. So, if we find ourself weak in our demonstration of the allness of good, we must hold that the good is all-powerful. It does not make any difference how powerful the evil may seem, you must hold to the Truth.

The poor people, the lame people, the deaf people, the sick people, do not disprove the proposition. I know that God is good, and good is all, and good is almighty. This knowledge, adhered to, will heal all apparent evils.

Add this idea to your mind and you will find that a certain clearness, a certain spiritual perception, and a *power* will come to you that you never have had before, because you are loyal to the Spirit of truth. With the realization of the almightiness of the good there may come to you the thought that all evil and all bad people should be destroyed at once. Very zealous Christians have been so possessed with this idea that they have given God the vengeful character of the Devil, instead of the Spirit of good.

Spirit of Love   Right here all Christians should know that the greatest idea in Divine Mind is love—"God is love."

When the Spirit of love begins to work in you, a soothing tendency, then a forgiving grace and charity will spring into your consciousness. The surest sign of the spiritual mind at work is forgiveness. You will love those who have despitefully used you. You will see unity in Spirit and strive to establish it in the world. If God should destroy all the evil people, what would become of the race? Why, there would not be a baker's dozen of us left! We should be like the man who wrote for prayer: "My wife and I do not get along together; please treat her."

Do not let the destructive idea, the idea of

burning up in hell-fire and the instant wiping out of all bad people, enter into your scheme of Truth. God is preserving His universe. He is redeeming it. He is educating it. And if we, in our overcoming, would fall into line with this patient regenerative process, which sets in just the moment that we perceive Truth, we must take every quality of God as revealed to us through Christ, and put it into execution in its right relation in Divine Mind.

Body Building   Truth is a healing force. Truth builds up the man. Truth restores the body. Some Christians have not fully perceived this. When Jesus Christ was accused of healing through the power of Beelzebub, He called attention to the inconsistency of the proposition, a "house divided against itself." Then He called particular attention to the restoring power of God; that God is the only good; that God heals man's bodies; that God is not the author of sickness.

God is not the author of evil in any of its forms. God is the author of health, and all health comes from God.

Unpardonable Sin   In Truth there is no such thing as an "unpardonable sin" but when we attribute our ills to God in the belief that they are sent upon us for some good purpose, we are committing a so-called "unpardonable sin." If you are under the thought that you have committed such a sin, just remember that the only way to be forgiven is to go to God and ask His forgiveness for your thought that He was the author of evil.

You must get into your own mind a clear idea of what the goodness of God is, and that that goodness extends into every department of your being. If there is any evil in you, it is the result of your own error thought. If you are sick, do not lay it to God. Do not lay any of your ill luck, your failures, or your shortcomings to God. Do not think for a moment that God has sent them upon you for a lesson.

Many people, good people, Christian people, sit down in humility and claim that God is giving them a lesson through some great trial, some great bodily illness. That is a grievous sin. So long as you continue in that attitude of mind, how can God forgive your errors and bring you back into the kingdom? You can see that all people who stick to such beliefs are beyond divine forgiveness.

 Change Your Mind　　　You must change your mind. You must realize that God, the good, demonstrates good only. Truth demonstrates itself in Truth. Know that God is the omnipresent good, and that when God occupies (as the Spirit of good) every part of your being, including your body, then the Spirit of truth from that moment begins to build you up. It restores your hearing. It strengthens your eyes. It heals your lameness. It makes whole every part of your body.

Do not let go of the proposition that God is the health of His people. God is infinite life. Hold to the Spirit of God, demonstrating itself in life everywhere.

That is what the scientific world is preaching today. We cannot get away from this proposition of the omnipresence of the one life. There is nothing else to come but the Spirit of truth. We do not look for another. We know that the Spirit of truth is here. It has always been here. We have turned our faces in another direction. We have looked somewhere else rather than to the Spirit of truth. The Spirit of truth is in the midst of you. It is in you. You will never have peace of mind, you will never have success in any way, you will never have health of body, you will never have anything satisfactory until you demonstrate its presence and its power in your life.

Would it not be well to think about this, right now? We are all striving for some ideal.

I never knew a man or a woman who failed to have an ideal deep within. Everyone desires to be something beyond his present achievement I tell you right now, you will never realize that ideal until you go into partnership with God. You must know Truth of Being. You must conform to Truth in every thought and in every act. Then you will have success. Then you will be satisfied. Then you will know that the Spirit of truth does demonstrate itself in man.

Secret of Satisfaction   Many passages from the Bible come to us without force because we apply them to a time beyond the grave instead of to the present life. One of these misapplied texts is: "When I awake, I shall be satisfied with beholding thy form." The realization of omnipresence puts meaning, substance, force, into this statement.

The foundation of the truth expressed in this text is written in the very beginning of the Scriptures. "Then God said, 'Let us make man in our image, after our likeness' . . . So God created man in his own image, in the image of God he created him; . . . And God saw everything that he had made, and behold, it was very good."

To awaken to the consciousness of this God-likeness is the secret of satisfaction. The degree of awakening measures the degree of satisfaction.

To be lost is simply to be unconscious of the divine perfection in man. This state of consciousness is ignorance, darkness, dissatisfaction, fear, and all that is pictured by the word *hell*. There is but one way to be saved from this condition and brought into heaven, or divine harmony, and that is through Christ, the perfect man, the only begotten, the image and likeness of God, the real self of every man.

Awakening comes from the quickening power of the word of Truth. Sense man is under a great many delusions, all arising out of the one great misunderstanding of the true character of man. The truth about himself will make him free.

Wisdom must be characteristic of man, since he is the image and likeness of God. If a man does not manifest wisdom, it simply shows that he is not awake to his true likeness. One must choose whether he wills to identify himself with the real self who knows, or with the natural, sense man who does not know.

Choice   Men do not always consider that the responsibility for this choice rests with them. Choose this day whom you will believe in as yourself. Choose Christ and serve

Him by identifying yourself with Him, in the face of appearances that deny you. This course will bring the quickening word of Truth into your consciousness, and you will be begotten by the Word and made a new creature in Christ.

The creature that you have seemed to be will no longer appear. The new man, image and likeness of God, will become manifest when you awaken to the consciousness of it. This new man does not appear all at once. His likeness must be held in mind in its absolute perfection or he will not appear at all.

The best way to prove that all wisdom and all understanding are in man is just to believe it to be true. Coming into the Christ consciousness is, in its first steps, all a matter of faith. The intellect, sense mind, thinks that it could understand if only somebody would explain Truth to it; but it never seems to understand.

The best way to prove this is to take some statement of Truth that is not clear. Hold it in mind. The power of the word will quicken the understanding, and light will flash from within. This is spiritual knowing.

Believe in the quickening power of the word. Hold the word in mind. It will reveal itself, for wrapped in the word is its meaning, and you, being the image and likeness of God, can understand it if you make connection with it in your inner consciousness. By planting it in consciousness and waiting for its fruit, anyone can prove that the word is seed.

The Eternal   Anything eternal has neither beginning nor end. We shall never get the realization of eternal life until we see it without beginning and without end. Jesus' words are a great help in awakening us in the likeness of the life that never began.

The demonstration of eternal life is open to everyone, but it cannot be made by anyone who identifies himself with the personal man and his limited concepts of life. Only he who awakens to the consciousness of himself as a son of God can have eternal life.

Selfishness has its stronghold in the personal man's claims upon the things that he loves. No one was ever permanently satisfied with personal love. Some of its fruit is bitter and its end is death. This may seem a hard saying, but it is true, and we might as well awaken at once to the love universal, in which is perfect satisfaction.

Hope of Satisfaction   We are awakening out of our dream and false hope of satisfaction in personal kinship, into the likeness of the God-love in which we feel the joy and the satisfaction of universal brotherhood.

This idea of awakening in the likeness of God might be carried out in all that we can conceive as belonging to the character of God. It will lift us out of negative conditions to consider His power and His strength and to awaken to His likeness in these attributes.

To be like Him in substance will clothe us with that glorified body which Jesus demonstrated. "Christ in you, the hope of glory" really means "Christ in you, the assurance of glory." The word *hope* is not strong enough; the glory is not in a far distant heaven, but within men— "Christ in you."

Living Faith

IF WE are wise, we shall cultivate faith in and understanding of omnipresent life. The man who is grounded in faith does not measure his thoughts or his acts by the world's standard of facts. Those who are in spiritual understanding know that faith has open eyes. Certain things do exist in Spirit and become substantial and real to the one who dwells and thinks and lives in faith. Such a one knows.

Concentrate on Faith   Faith is the foundation of all that man does. We should concentrate faith on the invisible, the real things, the things of Spirit.

How wonderful would be our demonstrations! How effective we should become in using the mighty power of Spirit!

We must raise our faith to the very highest in us and rest in the "assurance" or substance of its reality. Spiritual understanding reveals the universality of all things.

The word, the imagination, and faith work together. You must not only practice an idea; you must also give it form by infusing into it the substance of your living faith.

If you want to do the works of God, you must follow Christ. If you want to elevate yourself out of the physical, you must have faith in God and cultivate that faith through affirmation of your spiritual power and faith. The Lord's Prayer is continual affirmation from beginning to end.

Our Relation to God   We must have the understanding that our relation to God is that of a son to his father; that we exist in the one Mind as superman, even Christ. Man is the offspring of the Almighty. If the earthly child resembles its parents, how much more should the heavenly child resemble its Parent. The truth that God is the Father of man does away with the presumption that it is impossible for the finite to understand the Infinite. A sense of logic is a fundamental constituent of man's being. The science that is here set forth is founded upon Spirit. It does not conform to intellectual standards. Nevertheless, it is scientific.

Demonstration   There are three steps in every demonstration: the recognition of Truth as it is in principle; holding the idea; and acknowledging fulfillment. Pray believing that you have received, and you shall receive.

God is our resource. All things are provided for us by our Father. It is necessary to cultivate these ideas by considering them daily in all that we do. By prayer and meditation on words of Truth in the silence we may so open our consciousness to the inner divine presence that the necessary understanding, love, and power may be given us to enable us to bring forth in our own life the good results that we wish to see manifest. This is much better than waiting to see the demonstrations of others before believing and before attempting to bring forth demonstrations of our own. With the growth of faith in the mind of the individual there comes a quickening of all his thoughts by the influx of Truth. True faith in God separates itself from all negative beliefs.

God is never absent from you. He is constantly taking form in your life according to the exact pattern of your words, thoughts, and actions. Just as soon as you really bring your words and your expectations up to the measure of God's love for you, you will demonstrate.

Thoughts Are Seeds   Thoughts are seeds
                              that, when dropped
or planted in the subconscious mind, germinate, grow, and bring forth their fruit in due season. The more clearly we understand this truth the greater will be our ability to plant the seeds that bring forth desirable fruits. After sowing the plants must be tended. After using the law we must hold to its fulfillment. This is our part. God gives the increase. You must work in divine order and not expect the harvest before the soil has been prepared or the seed sown. You have now the fruits of previous sowings. Change your thought seeds and reap what you desire. Some bring forth very quickly, others more slowly, but all in divine order.

God does not do things in us against our will, as will acts in both the conscious and subconscious realms of mind. However much it may appear that the word is thwarted in its original intent, this is never true. It goes on and it enters where reception is given it.

Theory to Life   Each one of us must not only see the image of his desires as a theory, but he must also form it into a living, breathing thing through every motive and act of his life. If we have an idea, we must act just as if it were part of our life.

No man ever demonstrated his God-given powers in even a small way who did not help many others to do likewise. Preaching is good. Practice is better.

There is work for everyone who will listen to and obey the Spirit. That work is important, because it is eternal and brings results eternal in their nature. If you have heard the voice of the Lord and are obedient to it at any cost, you are chosen.

The kingdom of God is now existing right here in our midst. It is being externalized little by little. Whoever has a high, pure thought and affirms his allegiance to it as a part of his daily life is adding to the externality of that kingdom among men. Whoever affirms his allegiance to the good, regardless of all appearance of evil, and in dealing with his brother declares by word and act that only the good exists, is building white spires to the one and only true God.

We are the temples of God, of good. Through us is the light to shine, which is so bright as to dim the rays of those shining orbs of the night and the day.

We are all the chosen of the Lord. We make the covenant that carries us into His visible presence by laying down the personal man and taking up the universal man. He it is that thunders in the depths of our soul.

The Faith Faculty   The idea that faith is something that has to do only with one's religious experience is incorrect. Faith is a faculty of the mind that finds its most perfect expression in the spiritual nature. In order to bring out one's whole character it should be developed in all its phases. That it is a power is self-evident. People who have faith in themselves achieve far more than those who do not believe in their own ability. We call this self-faith innate confidence. Confidence is a form of faith. Belief is another of the expressions of faith.

In Spirit, faith is related to omnipresent substance or assurance. By meditation man lights up the inner mind, and he receives more than he can put into words. Faith can be extended in consciousness in every direction. It will accomplish wonderful things if quickened and allowed free expression in its native realm. Where faith is centered in outer things, the results are not worthy of mention. Men have named them luck, accident, chance, and the like. Such charms seem to work for a little while, then suddenly change, so it is evident that they are not under any enduring law.

Intellectual people do no miracles through faith. They limit its scope to what the intellect says is law. It is when faith is exercised deep in spiritual consciousness that it finds its right place, and under divine law, without variation or disappointment, it brings results that seemingly are miraculous. Perseverance is required in our use of faith until we make connection with the higher realms of consciousness.

Though our faith be as small as the smallest of seeds, it will spring forth and demonstrate its power to carry out every desire into which we infuse it.

Faith Seeing The power to see in Spirit is peculiar to faith. In its outer expression this power is sight; interiorly it is that which perceives the reality of the substance of Spirit. Mental seeing is knowing; we mentally discern.

Have faith in what you do. After it is done do not condemn yourself. We are all seeking happiness, contentment, and we know by experience that we are happy when we are in tune with our environment. There is a great variety of ideas that cause us inharmony. We think that if we have money and friends we can be happy; but things do not make happiness. It is our mental attitude toward things that fixes our relation to them. The better we understand the innate substance of the world about us, the more do we appreciate it.

Faith Ability   Faith is ever active. It should be made the truth substance of every idea. We should have faith in our own power, capacity, and ability. If we are to have this faith our thoughts must be centered in the great universal Mind. Success lies in God. Whatsoever is not of faith is sin. Whatsoever is of faith is not sin. Sin is a missing of the mark. We miss the mark by not having faith.

A very little faith often produces surprising results. The invisible forces are much closer than we think. When we turn our attention in their direction the response is usually so pronounced and so swift that we cannot but feel that a miracle has been performed. A more intimate acquaintance with the divine law convinces us that under it all things are possible if we only believe, and if we at the same time conform our thoughts to its principle.

We are constantly making conditions through our thoughts. In all our experience we

should condemn nothing that comes to us and
nothing that we do. We know the law. Let us
keep it and not set up any adverse conditions
by our thoughts of condemnation. Whatever you
are doing, be happy in it. You are getting the
results of your acts, according to your faith. Be
wise; pronounce nothing evil, and only good
will come.

Have faith in the innate goodness of all
men and all conditions. Do not condemn, no
matter how great the provocation. What you
think, you create in your own consciousness. En-
large your range of vision, and you may see
good in what now seems evil. God is good and
God is all, hence there can be no real condition
but the good. Why should we waste our time
fighting evil?

Faith-thinking   The most important power
                     of man is the original faith-
thinking faculty. We all have the thinking faculty located in the head, from which we send
forth thoughts, good, bad, and indifferent. If
we are educated and molded after the ordinary
pattern of the human family, we may live an
average lifetime and never have an original
thought. The thinking faculty in the head is
supplied with the secondhand beliefs of our
ancestors, the dominant beliefs of the race, or

the threadbare stock of the ordinary social whirl. This is not faith-thinking. Faith-thinking is done only by one who has caught sight of the inner truths of Being, and who feeds his thinking faculty upon images generated in the heart.

Faith-thinking is not merely an intellectual process, based upon reasoning. The faith-thinker does not compare, analyze, or draw conclusions from known premises. He does not take appearances into consideration. He is not biased by precedent. His thinking gives form, without cavil or question, to ideas that come straight from the eternal fount of wisdom. His perception impinges upon the spiritual and he knows.

When there has been an aspiration and a reaching out for the spiritual life, the faith faculty becomes active in consciousness. Spiritual faith includes unfailing assurance and immediate response. Faith in the reality of the invisible builds a real, abiding substance in the mind and in body. All kinds of ideas grow quickly when planted in this rich substance of the mind.

There is but one real faith. The avenue of expression determines the character and power of faith. Trust is a cheaper brand of faith, but trust is better than mistrust. People who merely trust in the Lord do not understand all the law. If they had understanding they would affirm the presence and power of God until the very substance of Spirit would appear in consciousness.

Faith Words   Faith words should be expressed both silently and audibly. The power of the spoken word is but slightly understood. The word is the creative idea in Divine Mind, which may be expressed by man when he has fulfilled the law of expression. All words are formative but not all words are creative. The creative word lays hold of Spirit substance and power.

The word of faith has an inner force. This force rushes forth and produces remarkable transformations in the phenomenal. It is not necessary that the one who touches faith shall understand all the intricate machinery with which he makes contact. Affirming the activity of this super-power will quicken it in consciousness.

Believing   If a man sanely believes he can do a thing he will eventually find a way to do it. The mind generates an energy that contacts the universal energy, and causes circumstances and events to fall into line for the attainment of the latent ideal. Tap this inner reservoir of faith, and you can do what Jesus did.

Belief is closely related to faith. It is an inner acceptance of an idea as true. Belief functions both consciously and subconsciously. Many false individual and race beliefs are very active below the conscious level. To erase these hidden error beliefs, a comprehensive program of denial is necessary.

Jesus' Faith   Jesus did not claim an exclusive supernatural power, which we usually accredit to Him. He had explored spiritual substance, which He called the "kingdom of the heavens." His understanding was beyond that of the average man. However, He knew and said that other men could do what He did if they would only have faith.

He encouraged His followers to take Him as a pattern for faith and to use the power of thought and word. Divine healing is due to the application of the same law that Jesus used. In most instances, He demanded faith on the part of those He healed. With this faith as a point of mental and spiritual contact, He released the latent energy in the atomic structure of the one in need of healing, and that one was restored to life and health.

Health

MAN, the apex of God's creation, was created in His image and after His likeness. Man is God's supreme creation. He may know God and become the vehicle and expression of God, the unlimited fount of life, health, light, and love. God is the health of His people.

The God Imprint   When Elohim God created man in His likeness, He imprinted upon man's supermind two body pictures: first the picture of a natural body, and second the picture of a spiritual body. In the primal cell He then enclosed the elements necessary to the building of the natural and the spiritual body.

To man was given dominion and authority

over these living atoms and cells out of which he must build mind and body into visibility. As God created man, His image and likeness, by the power of His word, so man, God's image and likeness, projects his body by the same power.

Our physical body is carried in our mind as thought and it obediently reflects every mental attitude. When in the course of our evolution we discern that an all-wise Creator must have designed perfection for all His creation and we begin to affirm that perfection, then the transformation from the natural to the spiritual body begins. It continues until our body is wholly regenerated and appears objectively in its divine perfection.

Object of Existence   The object of man's existence is to demonstrate the Truth of Being. This demonstration takes place through experience. There are two ways of working out experience. The first is by knowing the law of every process, and the second is by blindly testing the process without understanding the law. All experience develops personal identity—the consciousness of the power of Being in the self. This is the bringing forth of free will, which is inherent in all. In the course of his demonstrations of Being, man arrives at the place where he feels his own ability. He knows that he can exercise it without restraint.

The Human Body

Through man, God is forming or manifesting outwardly that which exists in the ideal. Every idea projects form. The physical body is the projection of man's consciousness. He carries the body in the mind. The body is the fruit of the tree of life which grows in the midst of the garden of mind. If the body-idea is grounded and rooted in Divine Mind, the body will be filled with a perpetual life flow.

The human organism has a world of latent energies waiting to be brought into manifestation. The human body is undoubtedly the most powerful dynamo in existence for the carrying on of life. By thought, speech, and deed the Christ Mind is brought into manifestation.

The body is made up of cells. The presiding ego of I AM in each organism determines the particular kind of impulse that the cells shall radiate. Some are in a radiant state. Some are in a crystallized form. The field of dynamic energy is limitless.

Crystallizing of these radiant thought forms is the result of affirmations in man's mind that his body is material instead of spiritual. The affirmative state of mind is a binding, holding process. It involves all thoughts and all thought manifestations that come within its scope. If man affirms his unity with the life, substance, and intelligence of God, he lays hold of these spiritual qualities. If he affirms the reality of matter and of the physical body he forms a material picture that works itself out in flesh.

Thought Builds   Thought is the builder of the body. The body is moved by thought. Thought not only moves the external members of the body, but it controls the fluids flowing within the body. Man's body has power to replace worn parts. When it is in harmony it never wears out. The harmony referred to is self-adjustment to the law of Being, to the law of divine nature, to the law of God. It does not matter what you call this fundamental principle underlying all life. The important thing is to understand it, and to put yourself in harmony with it. Nature is not a blind force working in darkness and ignorance. All her works indicate intelligence—mind in action.

Jesus is the outstanding pioneer in the realm where the health-producing processes of cells are released and imbued with supermind vitality. He spent years in becoming acquainted with His body, freeing its cells from the material bondage to which the race thought had bound them.

Birthright   Health is fundamental in Being and is man's divine birthright. To be healthy is natural. Health is the normal condition of man and of all creation. It is the orderly state of existence. It is a state of being sound or whole in mind, body, and soul. God's man is hale, whole, hearty.

Health, real health, is from within and does not have to be manufactured in the without. Health is the very essence of Being. It is as universal and enduring as God.

There is in man a capacity for knowing God consciously and communing with Him. Man must learn to use the knowledge of Truth to sustain his consciousness of health. This alone insures health, joy, and satisfaction.

To heal is to bring forth the perfect Christ man that exists within each of us. Christ in us is the little seed through which is brought forth the strong, healthy Christ man.

To know God as health one must take up the study of the healthy mind. When he lays hold of the principle of wholeness, he finds that he is automatically working with God and that much new power is added. He perceives principle working out his health problems for him.

By realizing a healing prayer man lays hold
of the principle of health itself and the whole
consciousness is illumined. When man becomes
so much at one with God-Mind that he abides
in the consciousness of health, he enters eternal
peace in which he knows that "it is finished."

Illness   There is but one body-idea. The
                 conditions in body express the
character of thought. The spiritual body of man
is the conception of Divine Mind, the creation
of Spirit for us. Our work is to make this spiritual body manifest.

A majority of the ills that afflict the body
have their origin in erroneous thoughts about
life. Man thinks his body into disease. Instead
of basing his thought on what is true in the
absolute of Being, he bases it on conditions as
they appear in the formed realm about him. The
result is bodily discord in multitudinous shapes.
Pervading all nature is a universal thought substance. Thought substance transcribes the slightest vibration of thought. The message is tran-
scribed and carried into action.

Sin   Jesus always connected sin and sick-
             ness as cause and effect. All the ills of
humanity are the effect of broken law, of sin.
That word *sin* covers more ground than we have

usually granted it. There are sins of omission and commission. If we fail to cultivate the consciousness of the indwelling spiritual life, we commit a sin of omission that eventually devitalizes the organism. To be continuously healthy we must draw on the one and only source of life, God. God is Spirit. Spirit pours its quickening life into mind and body when we turn our attention to it and make ourself receptive by trusting Spirit to restore us to harmony and health. The more enlightened man becomes, the greater his desire for health.

Sin is a missing the mark, a falling short of divine perfection. Sin is man's failure to express the attributes of Being. Sin (error) is first in mind and is redeemed by a mental process, or by going into the silence. Error is brought into the light of Spirit and then transformed into a constructive force.

Through the Christ Mind, our sins (wrong thinking) are forgiven or pardoned (erased from consciousness). When we have cast all sin (error thought) out of our mind, our body will be so pure that it cannot come under any supposed law of death or corruption.

Indulgence   Like a child who refuses to take the advice of one who knows, man falls into indulgence of the sense of pleasure and excess. The reaction of sense indulgence is pain. Through these experiences man comes into a consciousness of an opposite to the good. The dual mentality naturally sets up positive and negative forces in his mind. These opposing forces are reflected into the body.

Sin is the result of desire manifesting itself in erroneous ways. When the error is discovered and there is a willingness to correct it, under the law of forgiveness man erases it easily.

In spiritual understanding, the I AM of man forgives or "gives" Truth "for" error; then the mind is set in order and the body is healed.

Do not hold anyone in bondage to the thought of sin. If you do, it will pile up and increase in power according to the laws of mental action.

Right images become active through the power of thought. Man has unlimited power through thought. He can give his power to things or withhold it. If he thinks about the power of sin, he builds up and gives force to that belief until it engulfs him in its whirlpool of thought substance. He forgets his spiritual origin and sees only the human. Thus he thinks of himself as a sinner.

The way out of this maze of ignorance, sin, and sickness is through man's understanding of his real being, and then the forgiving or the giving up of all thoughts of the reality of sin and its effects in the body.

If anyone tries to free himself while holding others in the thought of sin, he will not demonstrate his freedom. You must build upon faith in the reality of the spiritual. Put your selfishness away. There cannot be two in this kingdom. It is the kingdom of God, and man must give up. The kingdom is for the larger man. The personal man must be eliminated.

Forgiveness Forgiveness really means the giving up of something. When you forgive yourself, you cease doing the thing that you ought not to do. Man has power to forgive sin. Sin is a falling short of the divine law. Repentance and forgiveness are the only means that man has of getting out of sin and its effect and coming into harmony with the law. All sin is first in the mind; the forgiveness is a change of mind or repentance. We forgive sin in ourself every time we resolve to think and act according to the divine law. The mind must change from a material to a spiritual base. Change must all be on the part of man and within him. The moment man changes his thoughts of sickness to thoughts of health the divine law rushes in and begins the healing work.

The law is Truth. The Truth is that all is good. There is no power and no reality in sin. If sin were real and enduring (like goodness and Truth), it could not be forgiven but would hold its victim forever.

Duty   Lack of health is not prevalent in God's universe. If such lack appears anywhere it is the work of man. It is our duty to do away with it. There is something wrong in a world where suffering and sorrow prevail. We would not create such a world. We all want to see these things blotted out in this world. This is the index pointing the way to the possibility of doing so. Just accept the promises of Scripture. Proceed to carry them out in faith. Act as if they were true. Trust God in all things. Whatever we see as wrong is for us to right. The new Christianity elevates man to a realm in which seeming miracles of healing become possible to those who train their mind to think spiritually.

Presence of Health   God is never absent from His creations. His creations are never absent from their habiliments. Wherever you see the evidences of life, there you may know that God is.

Health has a source that is perpetually giving itself forth. A perpetual giving forth implies a perpetual presence.

There is no absence or separation in God. His omnipresence is your omnipresence. There can be no absence in Mind. If God were for one instant separated from His creations, they would immediately fall into dissolution. In spirit and in truth you can never for one instant be separated from the life activity of God.

God lives in you. You depend on Him for every breath you draw. You could not think a thought or speak a word or make a movement were He not in it. Your body is the soil in which God's life is planted. Your mind is the light for which He supplies the oil.

Draw upon the omnipresent God for every need.

A good healing drill is to deny the mental cause first. Then deny the physical appearance. The mental condition should first be healed. Then the secondary state, which it has produced in the body, must be wiped out and the perfect state affirmed.

Nature and Health   We have been so persistently taught that nature heals that we do not as a rule give the question of the origin of her healing power any serious thought. If we center our attention on

nature as the healing principle, we stir up
natural activities that are secondary to the one
cause of all action, that is, infinite Mind. It is
our privilege as creations of supreme Mind to
bring into action all its forces, primary and
secondary. By our thought and the mighty mind
energy back of thought we can stir to action all
the power of Being and get the results of their
concentrated healing currents instead of the
weakened, segregated seepage from one.

Spiritual Healing   Nearly everyone needs
                              both mind and body
healing. Those who give faithful attention to
the law as it operates in man are rewarded by
demonstrations of healing.

Man and the universe are under the creative
direction of a supreme being. Man needs but to
conform to the laws of creative Mind in order to
be healthy, happy, and wise. All healing methods consist in establishing the unity of the individual and the universal consciousness. No
man heals himself or another. The supreme
Mind does the work.

The first step in all spiritual healing is to
believe. The next step is openness and recep-
tivity to the stream of healing life. Through the
exercise of faith and our words, our spiritual
quality is fused into unity with the power of

Christ and the work is marvelously accomplished.

All healing is based on mental cleansing. When the mind is free from error thoughts, harmony in the body ensues. Permanent healing is never accomplished until the mental cause of the disease, the error thought, is removed. The true way to heal is to find the mental cause and destroy it forever.

Consciousness and Health

Man's consciousness is formed of mind and its ideas. These determine whether he is healthy or sick. Mind is the common meeting ground of God and man. Only through its study and the observation of all the conditions and factors that enter into its operation can we come into the realization of God as abiding health and sustenance.

You are mind. Your consciousness is formed of thoughts. Thoughts form barriers about the thinker. You are compassed about with thought barriers, your heredity, your education, your own thinking. Your degree of health is determined by your thoughts, past and present. These thoughts may be true or false, depending on your understanding and use of divine law.

God created man in His image, in the image of perfect health. We make living cells through the imaging power of thought. We nourish a good thing by thinking how good it is. Suppose we take the negative side, shall we then get results also? Yes, absolutely! We get just what we think about. The thought of nourishing is a very good thought, because it shows us just what we do. Either we tear down our bodies or we build them up. Withdraw the error; then build in the good.

Processes of Mind   There is a definite relation between the thoughts of man and the conditions in his body. The body is moved by the mind. All the conditions of the body are brought about by the mind.

Jesus was the great teacher and example of obedience to the law of constructive thinking. The reform of Jesus is an inner transformation. If we follow Him we shall give our strength and substance and thought force to constructive activity. The movement of every mind in bringing forth the simplest thought is a key to the great creative process of universal Mind. In every act is involved mind, idea, and manifestation. The mind is neither seen nor felt; the idea is not seen, but it is felt; and the manifestation appears.

The mind functions in ways that are strange

and unbelievable. In order to understand God-Mind we need to study our own mind. The more we analyze the processes of the mind the more plainly the mind with its mental "compounds" appears as the source of health and of all other things. If we want to know the secrets of health and how right thinking forms the perfect body, we must go to the mind and trace step by step the movements that transform ideas of health into light, electrons, atoms, molecules, cells, tissues, and finally into the perfect physical organism.

We exist right in the midst of forces that would yield us power to do all our work if we knew how to utilize properly their energies. This is not only true of our use of the many elements in the natural world all about us but especially of our utilization of the energy generated by our mind. With every thought there is a radiation of energy. If a person is untrained in thinking and lets his mind express all kinds of thoughts without control, he not only used up thought stuff but fails also to accomplish any helpful result. Right thinking is using the mind to bring about right ends idealized by the thinker. Through concentration and conservation of thought force man regains consciousness of health in his mind, and health then becomes manifest in his body. Concentration, one pointed attention, forms a mental magnet in the mind to which thought substance rushes. Then follows confidence or faith in one's ability to accomplish the desired end. This is the law by which the universe was brought into manifestation.

To think is to express.

There is a chain of mind action connecting cause and effect in all the activities of life. This chain is forged by man, and its links are thoughts and words.

If I can conceive a truth, it follows that there is a way by which I can make it manifest. If I can conceive of omnipresent life as existing in the omnipresent substance, there is a way by which I can make that life appear in my body. No one ever fully sees the steps he is to take in reaching a goal. He may see in a general way that he is to go on from one point to another. The details are not definitely clear to him unless he has gone over the ground before. In demonstration of the spiritual powers that are ready to find expression through man he must be willing to follow the directions of one who has proved his efficiency by demonstration.

Faith   The blessing of health comes
               through the exercise of faith on the
part of the man who seeks it. Faith opens the

mind to the influx of power from on high. The power of the Highest heals all diseases both of soul and of body. When faith is sufficiently strong to dissolve all adverse conditions and to open the mind fully to the power of God, healing is instantaneous.

Through faith in the reality of things spiritual we begin soul evolution. We must have faith in Spirit and through our thinking build it into our consciousness. Then our body will be restored to harmony and health. In order to create as God creates, man must have undoubting faith in God-Mind and the obedience of the creative electrons hidden in the atoms of all substance. Although we all get definite results in body and affairs from the words we utter, those results would be infinitely greater if we understood the power of words and had undoubting faith in their creative power.

Imagination   Through the power of the imagination we impress upon the body the concepts of the mind. A man can imagine that he has some evil condition in body, and through the imaging law build it up until it becomes manifest. On the other hand, he can use the same power to make good appear.

Order   If we desire to demonstrate health
                 when we receive more spiritual life,
we must order this life rightly. If it is not so
ordered, mental and physical discord will en-
sue. This applies to all that we think and do.
Everything must be brought in order. There
must be order in the spiritual life as well as the
material life.

How can you order your life by the divine
plan? By accepting it as a truth that there is such
a plan and by making this plan yours through
affirming your oneness with the omnipresent
Mind in which this plan exists in its righteousness.

Ask for wisdom; then affirm divine order.
Put yourself in unity with Spirit. Then you will
come into the consciousness of a new world of
thought and act and find yourself doing many
things differently because the orderly Mind that
directs the universe is working through you. A
harmonious relation will be established in all
your ways.

Holding some disorganizing thought will
produce inharmony and discord in body and
affairs. Lack of orderly arrangement of thoughts
is responsible for many delayed demonstrations
of healing.

The bringing forth of man even in the material sense is an orderly process.

So long as we believe in the slow processes of what we call nature we shall place ourselves under a law of slowness.

Let us begin anew and lay down the law of order in all that we do. If there is a tendency to hurry, let us stop and affirm divine order and rest ourself in its poise. There is no need to hurry. You live in eternity now. This thought of omnipresent eternity will alleviate nervous tension. Put every thought and act under the divine law.

Healing Words   The usual conversation among people creates ill health instead of good health, because of wrong words. If the words speak of disease as a reality, disintegrating forces are set in action. These in the end shatter the strongest organism if not counteracted by constructive forces. The word of one in authority carries weight and produces far-reaching effects. Man has the power to deny and dissolve all disintegrating, discordant, and disease-forming words. Knowledge of this fact is the greatest discovery of all ages. You can make yourself a new creature.

Every word has within it the power to make manifest whatever man decrees. Spiritual words have this power. When one understands the power of words spoken in spiritual conscious-

ness the results are in fulfillment of divine law.
The quick and lawful way to attain health is to
put your creative words to work and bring into
swift action the superman Christ.

To understand the new life in Christ we
must give attention to that mystical Word, or
Logos. In it are wrapped the principles that,
planted in our mind, will spring into new life
in mind and body. Next to Spirit the Word of
Spirit is the most powerful thing in existence.
Man is the incarnate Word of God.

Our words bring forth whatever we put into
them. Words are quickened by those who speak
them. They pick up and carry the viewpoints of
the speaker, weak or strong, ignorant or wise,
good or ill.

One who heals by the power of the Word
should become familiar with the inner meaning
of all words and use those that appeal to him as
possessing the greatest healing potency.

Every word we speak goes forth from our
mouth charged with atomic energies. Our mind
determines the character of our words. What
the mind determines the mouth obediently ut-
ters. Its words are loaded with constructive or
destructive electrons all mathematically arranged to build up or blow up ourself, our aims,
and our ideals.

Some persons are overzealous. They consume their vitality by talking and acting without wisdom. They would find a much-coveted and needed poise by linking their minds with the Christ. Such persons are so enthusiastic in externals that they lose contact with the source of things. They destroy the body. However, these are the minority. The great majority lack zeal in doing even the most ordinary things.

When the mind of man is set on high, he never gives up or allows defeat to thwart his righteous ambitions. A failure state of mind throws the whole organism into a panic. Its functions are weakened in their life action. To one in spiritual understanding there is no loss. The going and coming of material and intellectual things are but changes in the panorama of life.

Thanksgiving   Thanksgiving will keep the heart fresh. True thanksgiving may be likened to rain falling upon ready soil, refreshing it and increasing its productiveness.

All things have their cause. Every cause is mental. Whoever comes in daily contact with a higher order of thinking cannot help but take on some of it. Ideas are catching. No man can live where true ideas of wholeness are being without becoming infected with them.

Words which express thanks, gratitude, and praise release energy of mind and soul. Their use is usually followed by effects so pronounced that they are quickly identified with the words that provoke them.

Let your words of praise and thanksgiving be of Spirit. The increase will be even greater than when they are addressed to man. The resources of Spirit are beyond our highest flight of imagination. You can praise a weak body into strength, a fearful heart into peace and trust, shattered nerves into poise and power.

It is an easy matter to give thanks for what we have already received. It is not so easy to give thanks for what we hope to receive. Giving thanks in advance brings to pass a present expectation. Pray believing that you have received, and you shall receive.

Praising and giving thanks liberate the finer essence of soul and body when we center our attention upon Spirit. Spirit is the dynamic force that releases the pent-up energies within man. The energies have been imprisoned in the cells and when released are again restored to action in the body by the chemistry of creative Mind. The perfection of this restoration is in proportion to the understanding and industry of the individual.

Every thought we loose in our mind carries

with it a certain substance, life, and intelligence. Whenever praise is bestowed it is carried to every part of the body and through a large area of our soul aura, and our whole consciousness and everything about us is tinctured with praise. Praise and thanksgiving divinely directed tap the mighty reservoirs of infinite Mind.

Joy   Nearly all persons have some pet fear. They give up to it without trying to find its source. There are various methods of erasing fear from the mind and preventing its congestions in the body. One of the most direct and effective shatterers of fear is laughter. Laugh your fears away. See how ridiculous they are when traced to their source.

We should cultivate those mind activities which stimulate naturally the currents of life in the body. Joy is a very important one. There is an intimate relation between happiness and health. When you feel good you sing, either audibly or silently. Singing promotes health because it increases the circulation. A good circulation is a sign and promoter of health. Nearly anyone can sing a little song. It is a marvelous health restorer. Singing restores harmony to tense nerves. Its vibrations stir them to action, thus making it possible for the ever-waiting healing Spirit to get in.

Back of every true song is a thought of joy. It is the thought that counts. It is the thought that invites the healing Spirit. We should sing with the thought that the Lord is right with us and that His joy is giving our words the healing unction.

When men think a great deal about spiritual things and especially about God as an indwelling spiritual presence, both mind and body are thrilled with joy, a feeling of satisfaction, and a tendency to break out in songs of gladness.

Everybody can sing. Cultivate the singing soul. Through the vibrations of the voice joined with high thinking every cell in the body is set into action, and not only in the body but out into the environing thought atmosphere the vibrations go and break up all crystallized conditions. The whole universe is in vibration. Vibration is under law. Each particular thing has its rate of vibration. What causes vibration? We answer: Mind.

Sing in your soul. You can sing 'way down inside yourself. Soon you will be singing with your voice. Persons everywhere, in every age, have told of an inner glory and happiness when they got into the habit of concentrating the mind on God.

Will   Every organ of the body is affected by the action of the will. Willfulness makes tenseness. A tense mind ties knots in the nerves, muscles, and tendons of the whole organism. Contrariness is another name for perverted will. Persons who are contentious for their personal rights place themselves in bondage to material conditions and stop spiritual growth. The will is not to be broken, but disciplined.

Peace   The Mind of Spirit is harmonious and peaceful. It must have a like manner of expression in man's consciousness. If we are not anchored to supreme and immovable reality, we shall be exposed to the storms of mortal thought and shipwrecked on the rocks of materiality. The mind may be compared to the sea, which is calm or stormy according to the wind that moves it. Thought utilizes the substance of the mind and forms that which man ideates. A restful state of mind is greatly to be desired because of its constructive character. When the mind is lashed by a brainstorm the cells of the whole organism are shattered and exhaustion ensues.

When a body of water is choppy with fitful currents of air it cannot reflect objects clearly. Neither can man reflect the steady strong glow

of Omnipotence when his mind is disturbed by
anxious, fearful, or angry thoughts.

Steadfast affirmations of peace harmonize
the whole body structure and open the way to
attainment of health conditions in mind and
body. Cast out enmity and anger and affirm
peace, and your healing will be swift and sure.
Be at peace, and your conscious unity with God-
Mind will bring you health and happiness.

Love   The word is the mind seed from
            which springs every condition. It is
the most enduring thing in existence. Words
make cells, and these cells are adjusted one to
the other through associated ideas. When divine love enters into man's thought process,
every cell is poised and balanced. Love over-
comes hate, resistance, opposition, obstinacy,
anger, jealousy, and all states of consciousness
where there is mental or physical friction.

Through the joining of the creative forces
of Spirit by souls attuned in love, the new body
in Christ is speedily formed. The work can be
done through individual effort. There must always be continuous constructive action between
the faculties of soul and body. If in quietness
and confidence the presence and the power of
divine love are affirmed, the law will be fulfilled.

Some of the most terrible ills are brought upon the body by the misuse of love.

Love wins when everything else fails. Nearly all sick people lack vital force, hence the life treatment is good for all. Hate, anger, jealousy, malice, and the like are almost universal in human consciousness, and a treatment for love will prove a healing balm for all.

Old Age   The marks of old age can be erased from the body by one's mentally seeing the body as youthful. If you want to be healthy, do not imagine so vain a thing as decrepitude. Make your body perfect by seeing perfection in it. The work must be an inner transformation. Actually old age is a false belief deeply embedded in the race mind. It accepts biological law as the ultimate for man instead of the law of God which is eternal life in the body.

Vitalization   We all need vitalizing. How shall we get life? What is the source of life? The life source is spiritual energy. It is composed of ideas. Man can turn on its current by making mental contact with it.

God is life and they who worship Him must worship Him in the life consciousness, that is, in Spirit. When we worship God in this way,

we are vitalized all at once. There is no other
way to get real, permanent life. We cannot get
life from the outer man or from anything external. We must touch the inner current.

We turn on the life current by means of
thoughts and words. We can have fullness of
life by realizing that we live in a sea of abundant, omnipresent, eternal life, and by refusing
to allow any thought to come in that stops the
consciousness of the universal life flow. We
live and move and have our being in Mind life.

You can think of your life as mental; every
faculty will begin to buzz with new life. Your
life will never wane if you keep in the consciousness of it as Mind or Spirit; it will increase and attain full expression in your body.
If you have faith in the life idea in your consciousness, your body will never be run down
but will become more and more alive with spiritual life.

We must think life, talk life, and see ourself filled with the fullness of life. When we are
not manifesting life as we desire, it is because
our thoughts and our conversation are not in
accord with the life idea. Every time we think
life, speak life, rejoice in life, we are setting
free, and bringing into expression in ourself,
more and more of the life idea. Here is the place
of abundant life, and we can fill both mind and

body, both our surroundings and our affairs, with glad, free, buoyant life by exercising faith in it.

Truth   Many have learned how to hold the truth about health steadily in faith even in the midst of the most adverse appearances. They clearly understand that they are not telling falsehoods when they deny sickness right in the face of the appearance of it. Persons who are quickened spiritually can do very much greater works through the law of faith than those who are still in the material consciousness. Once having discerned the power of Spirit, we should be on our guard and send forth on every occasion exalted ideas of the spiritual.

The one and only reason that we do not always succeed in our demonstrations is that we do not persist in our mental work. We must begin to discipline our mind and raise our thoughts to the point where they abandon the slow inertia of the natural man for the speed and spring of the spiritual man. This is accomplished by prayer, meditation, and the repetition of true words.

It is not the vain repetition of words over and over, parrotlike. It is the quiet realization that there is a listening Mind and a ready host of great ideas at all times waiting for us.

Praying for Others   One who prays for
                              the health of an-
other should understand that it is not the fault
of the healing principle that his patient is not
instantly restored. The fault may be in his own
lack of persistency or understanding; or it may
be due to the patient's dogged clinging to discordant thoughts. In any case the one who prays
must persist in this prayer until the walls of resistance are broken down and the healing currents are tuned in. In treating others see patients
as perfect.

Miracles   The universe was not created
                    through illogical assumptions of
law. Law is its foundation. There are no miracles in science. Jesus did no miracles. All His
marvelous works were done under the laws that
we may learn and use as He did. As the body is
moved by mind, so the mind is moved by ideas.
Right here in the mind we find the secret of the
universe.

In reality miracles are events that take place
as a result of the operation of a higher, unknown
law. All true action is governed by law. Nothing just happens. All happenings are the result of cause and can be explained under the
law of cause and effect.

Mighty things have been wrought in the past by those who had mere blind faith to guide them. To faith we now add understanding of the law.

Jesus Christ   Quite a few Truth students ask why we emphasize Jesus Christ so strongly in our writings and statements of Truth. Spiritual psychology proves that the name of a great character carries his mind potency. Wherever his name is repeated silently or audibly his attributes become manifest.

We are all, in our personality, wearing the mask that conceals the real, the spiritual, I AM. Any declaration man may make in which the name *Jesus Christ* is used reverently will contact the Christ I AM and will open the mind and body to the inflow of spiritual healing rays. When man thinks or says "I am" he is potentially giving freedom to the seed ideas that contain in their spiritual capacity all of Being. The natural man in his narrowed mental comprehension barely touches the seed ideas that expand in the Christ man to infinite power. The more we dwell upon and expand our I AM the greater looms its originating capacity before us. The Christ substance and the Christ life are accessible at all times and in all places to the one who awakens his I AM to spiritual omnipresence.

Proofs   We find as we study and apply the
                doctrine of Jesus that our body
must be included. Faith in the omnipresent pure
substance precipitates the substance in the body
and we are transformed.

Proofs may be found in profusion that the
divine law of body restoration is in action in a
large way right here in our midst. The litera-
ture of Unity teems with testimonials of persons
who have been healed and are grateful to God
for renewed health, strength, prosperity, and
happiness. Thus it is not necessary to strengthen
your faith by reading about the work of God
in ages past; you can personally consult your
neighbor, who can doubtless tell you of marvels
fully as great as any recorded in the Bible.

The majority of cases that come to us belong to the class of the discouraged woman told
of in Luke 8:43 (A.S.V.), "who spent all her living upon physicians, and could not be healed."
Doctors have pronounced them incurable, and
as a last resort they turn to God. The hardest
part of the work in their healing is to get out
of mind the verdict of doctors that their cases
are incurable. We have discovered that there are
no incurables. Any experienced metaphysical
healer will tell you that he has been the instru-

ment through which all the "popular" diseases have been healed.

Personal Testimony   When a boy of ten I was taken with what was at first diagnosed as rheumatism but developed into a very serious case of hip disease. I was in bed over a year, and from that time an invalid in constant pain for twenty-five years, or until I began the application of the divine law.

Two very large tubercular abscesses developed at the head of the hip bone, which the doctors said would finally drain away my life. But I managed to get about on crutches, with a four-inch cork-and-steel extension on the right leg. The hip bone was out of the socket and stiff. The leg shriveled and ceased to grow. The whole right side became involved; my right ear was deaf and my right eye weak. From hip to knee the flesh was a glassy adhesion with but little sensation.

When I began applying the spiritual treatment there was for a long time slight response in the leg, but I felt better, and I found that I began to hear with the right ear. Then gradually I noticed that I had more feeling in the leg. Then as the years went by the ossified joint began to get limber, and the shrunken flesh filled out until the right leg was almost equal to the other.

Then I discarded the cork-and-steel extension and wore an ordinary shoe with a double heel about an inch in height. The leg became almost as large as the other, the muscles were restored.

I am giving minute details of my healing because it would be considered a medical impossibility and a miracle from a religious standpoint. However I have watched the restoration year after year as I applied the power of thought, and I know it is under divine law. So I am satisfied that here is proof of a law that the mind builds the body and can restore it.

Music and Healing

THE healing power of music, which is heralded as a modern discovery by those who are practicing it in hospitals, is not new. The fact is, this method of healing has always been recognized and practiced, the most striking illustration being the universal lullabies which mothers, civilized and savage, sing to soothe their tired children. In every nation, and in every tongue, the lullaby has its place. We assume that every child has been harmonized mentally and physically by the mother's song, however crude that song may have been.

Harmonious Ideas   Metaphysicians have
                            discovered that a har-
monious arrangement of ideas in mind produces harmony in body; that within the five
avenues of expression, called the senses, there
are certain thoughts that can be adjusted one to
another. The mind and body can be filled with
such harmony that a song of joy springs forth
without volition. This relation is governed by
an exact science, and works out the same way
every time.

The relation is similar to the mathematical
accuracy which governs the arrangement of
tones in musical harmony. Ideas, mathematics,
and music are related. When the mind understands that relation and applies it the harmony
called health follows.

Pythagoras went to Egypt, and stayed there
twenty-one years learning occultism. When he
returned to his home, he preached some strange
doctrines. He said that man and the whole universe were created as a musical production.

Musical Vibration   If dry sand is placed
                            on a plate and a violin
bow is drawn across the plate, the sand will
arrange itself in symmetrical forms. Probably
the earth took form from the harmonious vibrations of the Word, and it may be that God is

singing the universe into expression this moment.

The most wonderful music box in the world is man's body. There are reeds and bellows and pipes. The whole physical organism seems to have for its purpose the production of sweet sounds. Who can tell what he may do when all his forces are brought into play and he knows how to control them properly?

When the faculties are in spiritual harmony, music flows from man as naturally as the brook murmurs in cadence or Niagara roars in organ tones. A free, unburdened mind naturally expresses itself in some sort of music; for example, the whistling boy.

A poet says that the man who has no music in his soul is fit for treason, stratagem, and spoils. It is universally observed that people who live on the seamy side of life seldom express themselves in song. An employer of wide experience once said that he always trusted the man who hummed or whistled at his work.

Seven Tones God is the universal Spirit of harmony. Man is the offspring of that Spirit. We have seven centers that correspond to the seven tones of the musical scale. When these seven tones are in harmony, like an aeolian harp the Spirit plays tones in your body if you will study them.

In the head is intelligence. It is "do." I AM is the keynote. Next is power, then come love, substance, order, life, strength. Each of these has a ganglionic center in the body. It makes a great difference how you play on them. If you believe in weakness and failure, your voice will express that belief. You have let go of your power center. How may you key it up? By going to the Source of power, and affirming your oneness with it. Declare that you have power to express in all its fullness your Christ mastery and dominion. Think of all the power of the universe centered at your throat. Sing songs of victory. Raise your voice in praise, and you will lift your whole organism into high, harmonious spiritual radiation.

When you know this law, you will know just how to tone up your body. When thoughts are making it lax or tense so that it cannot sound forth divine harmony, you can speak the true, freeing, toning-up word, and put yourself in tune, within and without.

Spirit of Music   The spirit of music is within all of us. When we have developed and brought it forth; when the quickening, harmonizing life has entered the physical, by the union of God with man, then we will realize that there is a power in us which will produce harmony. And harmony is health.

So we see that the body is a musical instrument, meant to give forth the harmony of Divine Mind. It must therefore be kept in tune with the Infinite. We need to learn how to put it in tune, keep it in tune, and how to play upon it, and this is all done by right thinking and right speaking. Thinking in wisdom produces harmony of mind and grace of body. All discord is produced by ignorant, unwise thoughts and words.

Healing by Music In time, probably, there will be schools of healing based on music, where patients will be taught how to center themselves in the harmonious Christ mind. The body will then respond, for it is mind, has its foundation in mind, lives in mind, and is moved upon by mind. The more we think about the great pulsating, universal life, the more we shall express it.

We may apply music in every department of life. The body is not only a musical instrument, it is also the composition. You are constantly composing as well as playing.

As you come into the harmony of Divine Mind, you will be able to play above and below the staff, and your ear will be quickened far beyond its present range of hearing. You will hear, not only the music of the spheres, but you will be able to discern musical tones in what now seems to be merely noise. The whir of the dynamo is the music of a bass viol; in the traffic of the street you will catch a deep musical tone, and when you are in perfect harmony in thought, you will hear music everywhere.

Time and Music   As time in music is mere-
                          ly a measure of pulsa-
tions, so years are measures of events. Time, therefore, being but a measure, is under your control. You can diminish or increase the movement at will. You can crowd into one year experiences that will make it seem like a hundred. This understanding that you are not in bondage to time, but that you control it, gives you a sense of freedom and your life's music will have fuller and better expression. You will not play mechanically, but your soul will be free to express its own harmony.

Bring harmony into your life by singing and praising. Everybody should play and sing. We should rejoice in the divine harmony. We should sing songs of joy and of love and of peace and of the unity of the Spirit, the Spirit of Jesus Christ, the supreme Man expressed.

Disease

IT IS NOW almost universally accepted by physicians that the majority of diseases are caused by minute forms of life commonly called germs. Each disease has its specific germ. They may be seen with very strong microscopes, and the form and the character of the different varieties are described by experts.

The antidotes for these destructive little germs have been widely advertised. The remedies consist in destroying them. They do not attempt to explain their origin. They find the little worker busy in the bodies of mankind, and they seek to put it out of action, not asking whence it came nor whither it may go.

The reflective mind is not satisfied with this superficial way of dealing with such destructive agents. It asks their cause, but no answer is vouchsafed on the part of those who study them. Only the students of mind can answer the question of the origin of disease germs. Only in terms of mind can there be given a rational explanation of these minute life forms.

The Adam man, the intellect, is responsible for them. He gives character to all the ideas that exist—he "names" them. This process is intricate, and it may be explained and understood in its details only by metaphysicians of the deepest mental insight. It is summed up in what is commonly called thinking.

Thoughts Produce Thoughts of health produce germs whose office it is to build up healthy organisms. Thoughts of disease produce germs of disorder and destruction. Here we have the connecting link between *materia medica* and metaphysics. The physician observes the ravages of the disease germ. The metaphysician stands in the factory of mind and sees thoughts poured into visibility as germs. This opens up a field of causes unlimited in extent. Every thought that flits through the mind of every man, woman, and child in the universe produces a living organism, a germ of a character like its producing thought. There is no escape from this conclusion, no escape from the mighty possibilities of good and ill that rest with the thinker.

Following Directions   Anger, jealousy, malice, avarice, lust, ambition, selfishness, and in fact all of the detestable patterns that mankind harbors, produce living organisms after their kind. If we had microscopes strong enough, we should find our body to be composed of living germs, doing to the best of their ability the tasks which our thoughts have set before them.

If you have said, "I hate you," there have been created in your atmosphere hate germs that will do the work for which you created them. If one's enemies alone were attacked by these germs of thought, the law would not be so severe, but they have no respect for anyone, and are likely to turn upon the body of their creator and tear it down.

So the fear, the doubts, the poverty, the sin, the sickness, the thousand erroneous states of consciousness have their germs. These organisms whose office it is to make men miserable do their work to the very best of their ability. They are not responsible for their existence. They are the formed vehicles of thought. They are the servants of those who gave them life. It is not to the germs that the wise regulator of affairs should look, but to those who are creating them and thereby bringing into existence discord and disease.

Counterfeit   Remedies beyond number are advertised for germs. They are guaranteed to kill the germ only. What is needed is a medicine that will prevent its appearance. To apply the remedy to the poor little germ is like trying to stop the manufacture of counterfeit money by destroying all that is found in circulation.

All counterfeit thought comes from the intellect, which alone originates the disease germ. We need to go no further than the disobedient intellect to find the cause of all the ills to which humanity has become slave. Wisdom is not an attribute of the intellect. The assumption that its observations are a source of wisdom is the one thing against which the Lord God especially warned Adam. This very clearly indicates the inability of the intellect, on its own account, to set up a standard of knowledge of good and evil. It also declares the end to which man will come if he disregards the prohibition specified.

"But of the tree of the knowledge of good and evil you shall not eat, for in the day that you eat of it you shall die."

Good and Evil   That there is something wrong in the present standard of good is evidenced by the variety of opinions in the world as to what is good and what is evil. There should be no question on such vitally important points. There would not be if the intellect would relinquish its claim to a knowledge of good and evil, and would relegate to Spirit the offices of wisdom and understanding.

The intellect is the formative, character-giving mechanism in the man. It draws its substance and intelligence from the Spirit. Like the prism through which the ray of white light is passed, it shows the potentialities of Spirit. If it looks within and seeks the guidance of Spirit, it reflects divine ideas upon the screen of visibility. This is the plan that the Lord has for it, and it is building according to that plan only when it admits that there is a higher source of wisdom than itself, when it submits to wisdom, for approval or disapproval, the ideas that it conceives.

Manifestation   The manifestation of life is through the Adam consciousness, which is, in a way, attached to and responsible for the forms thus made visible. Hence the reform—the transformation—of existing conditions must be made from the standpoint of Adam as an important factor. To ignore Adam is to slight one of the established creations of Jehovah God. If Adam were not a part of the divine plan, why was he formed from the dust of the earth, the breath of life breathed into him, and a living soul capacity given to him?

We are not to erase Adam. We are to transform him. He is not a safe guide in anything. His conclusions are derived from observation of conditions as he sees them in the external world. He judges according to appearance, which is but one side of the whole. Appearances say that germs are dangerous and destructive, but one who is familiar with their origin is not alarmed. He knows that there is a power and wisdom stronger and wiser than the ignorant intellect. It is to this power that we are compelled to go before we can right the wrongs that now dominate the mind of man. There is but one fount of wisdom, and that is wisdom itself.

Wisdom   The belief that wisdom is attained through the study of things is an error prevalent in this age. They

who wait upon the Lord shall be wise. That the
wisdom of health can be evolved from the study
of disease germs is a concept of the intellect in
its tendency to look without instead of within.
The without, the universe of things formed, is
not and never can be a source of wisdom. The
things formed are the result of efforts to com-
bine wisdom and love, and their character indicates the success or the failure of the under-
taking. When wisdom and love have been invoked, and their harmony has been made manifest in the thing formed, God is manifest.

We love to name or give character to the
ideas of Jehovah God, because it is our office in
the grand plan of creation to do so. The glory
of the Father is thus made manifest through the
Son. In no other way can the ideas in Being be
made manifest, and man should rise to the dignity of his office and formulate them according
to the plans of Divine Mind.

Disease germs would quickly disappear
from the earth if men would consult God before passing judgment upon His creations. It is
not man's province to give form to anything but
what will be a pleasure in God's eye. If he
makes germs it is because he thinks germ
thoughts. When he thinks God thoughts he
will form only the beauties of nature and mankind, and there will no longer be anything in

all his world that will cause a fear or a moment of pain. God is not the author of this condition of so-called "progress from matter to mind." God is the one source from which and of which man makes his existence.

Unfoldment   There is a law of unfoldment in Being, a law as exact as the progressive steps in a mathematical problem in which no error is made, a law as harmonious as that which governs a musical production where discord has found no place. Disease germs are not a part of the divine law. They are as far removed from it as would be error in the steady, careful steps in the progressive unfoldment of numbers, or false notes in symphony or song.

It does not require labored arguments or hard thinking to see how easily the problems of life would be made orderly and divine if men would let the Lord into his mind. Jesus said that the yoke was easy and the burden light. He was victor over all the hard conditions to which men and women yoked themselves. He made light of sin, disease, and poverty, by annulling them and preaching boldly in the face of an adverse theology that it was the prerogative of the Son of man to blot these errors from the world of mankind.

Royal Road There is a royal road for every man—a road in which he will be conscious of the dominion that is his by divine right. That road, Jesus said, leads out from the I AM. As Moses delivered the Children of Israel from the Egyptian darkness of their ignorance by affirming in their ears the power of the I AM, so Jesus gives us a series of affirmations that will deliver us from the wilderness of ignorance.

Your I AM is the polar star around which all your thoughts revolve. Even the little, narrow concept of the personal "I am" may be led out into the consciousness of the great and only I AM by filling its thought sphere with ideas of infinite wisdom, life, and love. Your I AM is that which carries you up or down, to heaven or to hell, according to the concept to which you have attached it. Hitch it to a star. Let it carry you to the broad expanse of heaven. There is room aplenty. You will not knock elbows with anyone if you get out of the surging crowd and hitch your I AM to the star of spiritual understanding.

Disease Antidote Cease making disease germs. Turn your attention to higher things. Make love alive by thinking love. Make wisdom the light of the world by affirming God's omnipresent intelligence. See in mind the pure substance of God, and it will surely appear. This is the way to destroy disease. This is the antidote for disease germs. The real, the enduring things of God are to be brought into visibility in just this simple way. This is the way in which the I AM makes itself manifest. The method is so easy that the man of great intellect passes it by. It is so plain that a simpleton may understand it. One does not have to know about anything whatsoever except God. How easy it is: how light the burden! No long, tedious years of study, no delving into depths of intricate theories and speculations are necessary. All that is required is a simple, childlike attention directed to the everywhere present Spirit, and a heart filled with love and goodness for everything.

Prosperity

THE teachings of Jesus stand out prominently, because they can be applied practically to the affairs of everyday life. His is not a religion in the sense that this word is usually taken but is a rule of thinking, doing, living, and being. To some people it is unthinkable to connect His teachings with the countinghouse and the market place. Deeper insight into their meaning and purpose shows that these lofty teachings are the most practical rules for daily living in all departments of life. They are vital to modern civilization and the very foundation of business stability.

We have not been more successful in making the teachings of Jesus a practical standard for everyday guidance because we have not understood the laws on which they are based. Jesus would not have put forth a doctrine that was not true and not based on unchanging law.

Men have taken the letter or appearance side of Jesus' doctrine and materialized it to fit their beliefs and customs. That is the reason why His message has not purified commerce, society, and government. It should be made spiritually operative in those fields. It will easily do the work desired when its mental side is studied and when it is understood and applied from the spiritual viewpoint. No permanent remedy will ever be found for the economic ills of the world outside a practical application of the laws on which the doctrine of Jesus Christ is based.

The Provider   It is perfectly logical to assume that a wise and competent Creator would provide for the needs of His creatures in their various stages of growth. The supply would be given as required and as the necessary effort for its appropriation was made by the creature. Temporal needs would be met by temporal things, mental needs by things of like character, and spiritual needs by spiritual elements. For simplification of distribution all would be composed of one primal spiritual substance, which under proper direction could be transformed into all products at the will of the operator.

Jesus taught that we can incorporate life-giving rays into our mind, body, and affairs through faith. He taught man how by the exercise of his mind he can make that life obey him. Instead of a universe of blind mechanical forces Jesus showed the universe to be persuaded and directed by intelligence.

What we need to realize above all else is that God has provided for the most minute needs of our daily life, and that if we lack anything it is because we have not used our mind in making the right contact with the supermind and the cosmic ray that automatically flows from it.

New Era　　We are now in the dawn of a new era. Old methods of supply and support are fast passing away. New methods are waiting to be brought forth. In the coming commerce man will not be a slave to money. Humanity's daily needs will be met in ways that are not now thought practical. We shall serve for the joy of serving, and prosperity will flow to us and through us in streams of plenty. The supply and support that love and zeal will set in motion are not as yet largely used by man.

The very air is alive with dynamic forces that await man's grasp and utilization. These invisible, omnipresent energies possess potentialities far beyond our most exalted conception. Truly, all things have their source in the invisible spiritual substance.

In the new era that is even now at its dawn we shall have a spirit of prosperity. The principle of universal substance will be known and acted on. There will be no place for lack. Supply will be more equalized. There will be no overproduction or underconsumption or other inequalities of supply, for God's substance will be recognized and used by all people. Men will not pile up fortunes one day and lose them the next, for they will no longer fear the integrity of their neighbor nor try to keep their neighbor's share from him.

Is this an impractical utopia? The answer depends on you. Just as soon as you individually recognize omnipresent substance and put your faith in it, you can look for others around you to do the same. When even one bears witness to the truth of the prosperity law he will quicken the consciousness of the whole community.

The Heavens   According to the Greek, the
                     language in which the New

Testament has come to us, Jesus did not use the word *heaven* but the word *heavens* in His teaching. He was not telling us of the glories of some faraway place called "heaven" but was revealing the properties of the "heavens" all around us. He taught not only its dynamic but also its intelligent character, and said that the entity that rules it is within man. He told His followers that it was the kingdom from which God clothed and fed all His children. In His many parables and comparisons referring to the "heavens" Jesus was explaining to His hearers the character of the omnipresent substance that has all potentiality and is the source of everything that appears on the earth. The kingdom of the heavens, or the kingdom of God, is within man. It is a kingdom of substance and of Mind.

Mind   All is Mind. The things that appear are expressions of Mind. Mind is reality, and it also appears as phenomena. The is-ness of mind is but one side of it. Being is not limited to the level of is-ness. It has all possibilities, including that of breaking forth from its inherencies into the realm of appearances. Mind has these two sides, being and appearance, the invisible and the visible. To say that mind is all and yet deny that things do appear to have any place in the allness is to state but half the truth.

Substance   God is substance. If by this
                     statement we mean that God is
matter, a thing of time or condition, then we
should say that God is substanceless. God is not
confined to that form of substance which we
term matter. God is an intangible essence. Matter is a mental limitation of the divine substance
whose vital and inherent character is manifest
in all life expression. God substance may be
conceived as God energy, or Spirit light.

God is substance, not matter, because matter
is formed, while God is the formless. God substance lies back of matter and form. It is the
basis of all form yet does not enter into any
form as a finality. Substance cannot be seen,
touched, tasted, or smelled, yet it is more substantial than matter, for it is the only substanti-
ality in the universe. Its nature is to "*sub*-stand"
or "stand under" or behind matter as its support
and only reality.

Inexhaustible Mind substance is available
at all times and in all places to those who have
learned to lay hold of it in consciousness. Spiritual substance from which comes all visible
wealth is never depleted. This unfailing resource is always ready to give. It has no choice
in the matter; it must give, for that is its nature.

Spiritual substance is a living thing. It is living bread and living water. He who feeds on God's substance shall never hunger and never thirst. This substance is an abiding thing. It is an unfailing principle that is sure in its workings. Man can no more be separated from his supply of substance than life can be separated from its source.

Ideas   Substance exists in the realm of ideas
                 and is power when handled by one
who is familiar with its characteristics. The ideas of Divine Mind are contained potentially in substance. All things exist as ideas. These ideas are manifested only as man becomes conscious of them. Divine ideas are man's inheritance. They are pregnant with all possibility. All the ideas contained in the one Father-Mind are at the mental command of its offspring. Get behind a thing, into the mental realm where it exists as an inexhaustible idea, and you can draw upon it perpetually and never deplete the source.

Unification   Substance is first given form
                    in the mind. You have doubtless in your own experience caught sight of the everywhere present substance in your silence, when it seemed like golden snowflakes were

falling all about you. This was the first manifestation from the overflow of the universal substance in your consciousness.

Be still and turn within to the great Source. See with the eye of faith that the whole world is filled with substance. See it falling all about you as snowflakes of gold and silver. In laying hold of substance in the mind and bringing it into manifestation, we play a most important part. Man's work is to express substance ideas in material form. Identify yourself with substance until you make it yours.

Actually, you are unified with the one living substance, which is God, your all-sufficiency. From this substance you were created. In it you live and move and have your being. By it you are fed and prospered.

Spiritual substance is steadfast, immovable, enduring. It does not fluctuate. It does not decrease.

As you lay hold of substance with your mind, make it permanent and enduring. Realize your oneness with it. Then you will soon begin to rejoice in the ever-present bounty of God.

Law   All true action is governed by law. Nothing just happens. There are no miracles. There is no such thing as luck. Nothing comes by chance. All happenings are the result of cause and can be explained under the law of cause and effect. This is a teaching that appeals to the innate logic of our mind. We sometimes feel like doubting it when we see things that have no apparent cause.

Happenings that seem miraculous are controlled by laws that we have not yet learned and result from causes that we have not been able to understand.

Man does not demonstrate according to the law but according to his knowledge of the law. That is why we must seek to learn more of it. What are the rules of the law? First, God is good and all His creations are good. When you get that firmly fixed in your mind, you are bound to demonstrate good, and nothing but good can come into your world. If you let in the thought that there is such a thing as evil and that you are as liable to evil as to good, then you may have conditions that conform to what you believe about evil.

Those who live in accordance with the law will get the desired results. Those who fail to do so will get the opposite results. The law applies to our demonstrations of prosperity.

God is law and God is changeless. God has ordained the law but does not compel us to follow it. We have free will. The manner of our doing is left entirely to us. When we know the law and work with it, we are rewarded by its protection and use it to our good.

The Father's desire (law) for us is unlimited good, not merely the means of a meager existence. The Father gives us all that He has and is when we return to the consciousness of His house of plenty. We cannot be happy if we are poor. Nobody needs to be poor. It is a sin to be poor. It is a sin to wear poor clothes.

The law cannot fail to operate when once set in operation in the right way. All men who have prospered used the law, for there is no other way. Perhaps they were not conscious of following definite spiritual methods, yet they have in some way set the law in operation and reaped the benefit of its unfailing action. Others have to struggle to accomplish the same things.

You will not have to wait for seedtime and harvest when you learn to use the power of your mind. When you have the consciousness in which your ideas are tangible, all your demands will be quickly fulfilled by the higher law. Throw into your ideas all the life and power of your concentrated thought, and they will be clothed with reality.

Your conscious cooperation is necessary to the fullest results in the working of the universal law of increase. Use your talent, whatever it may be, in order to increase it. Have faith in the law. Do not reason too much but forge ahead in faith and boldness. If you let yourself think of any person or any outer condition as hindering your increase, this becomes a hindrance to you. Keep your eyes on the abundant inner reality. Do not let the outer appearance cause you to falter.

Consciousness The possessions of the Father are not in stocks and bonds but in the divine possibilities implanted in the mind and soul of every man. Through the soul of man God's wealth finds its expression. Wealth of consciousness will express itself in wealth of manifestation. One who knows Principle has a certain inner security given him by the understanding of God-Mind.

In order to demonstrate Principle we must keep establishing ourself in certain statements of the law. Affirmations are for the purpose of establishing in our consciousness a broad understanding of the principles on which all life existence depends. The more often you present to your mind a proposition that is logical and true, the stronger becomes that inner feeling of security to you.

Housecleaning A mental housecleaning is more necessary than a ma-

terial one, for the without is but a reflection of
the within. Old thought must be denied and the
mind cleansed in preparation before the affirmative Christ consciousness can come in. When
we consistently deny the limitations of the material, we begin to reveal the spiritual law that
waits within us to be fulfilled. When this law is
revealed to our consciousness, we begin to use
it to demonstrate all things that are good.

Loose all thoughts of lack and lay hold of
thoughts of plenty. See the abundance of all
good things. We live in a very sea of inexhaustible substance, ready to come into manifestation
when molded by our thought.

No step in spiritual unfoldment is more important than renunciation or elimination. We
must learn to let go, to give up, to make room
for the things we have prayed for and desired.
It is simply giving up and casting away old
thoughts that have put us where we are, and
putting in their place new ideas that promise to
improve our condition. There must be a constant elimination of the old to keep pace with
growth. When we cling to the old we hinder
our advance or stop it altogether.

Denial sweeps out the debris and makes
room for the new tenant that is brought into
the mind by the affirmation. It would not be
wise to eliminate the old thoughts unless you

knew that there were higher and better ones to take their place.

Rewards   Those who seek the things that the material realm has to offer usually find them. Those who aspire to spiritual rewards are also rewarded. The law is that we get what we want and work for. Where there is no reward for effort, there will be no effort, and society will degenerate. We may talk about the inner urge, but when it has no outer field of action it eventually becomes discouraged and ceases to act.

Effort   If your prosperity does not become manifest as soon as you pray and affirm God as your substance, your supply, and your support, refuse to give up. A continuity of effort is necessary. Show your faith by keeping up the work. You do not have to work laboriously in the outer to accomplish. Most of us rush around trying to work out our problems for ourself and in our way, with one thought, one vision: the material thing we seek. You need to devote more time to silent meditation. Remember that substance ideas with which you are working are eternal. The same ideas that formed this planet in the first place sustain it now.

Faith   The subject of faith should be ap-
              plied especially to the demonstra-
tions of prosperity. It is our starting point in
building a prosperity consciousness and making
our world as we would have it. We all have
faith, for it is innate in every man. Our question
is how we may put it to work in our affairs.

In a sense faith represents substance. With
it, it is possible to possess a reality that cannot
be seen, touched, or comprehended by any of
the outer senses. It is faith when we are fully
conscious of "things not seen" and have the
"assurance of things" not yet manifest. In other
words, faith is that consciousness in us of the
reality of the invisible substance and of the
attributes of mind by which we lay hold of it.
We must realize that the mind makes things
real.

"Just a thought" or "just a mere idea," we
sometimes lightly say, little thinking that these
thoughts and ideas are the eternal realities from
which we build our life and our world.

The foundation of every work is an idea.
Faith is that quality of mind which makes the
idea stand out as real, not only to ourself but to
others. When others have faith in the thing you
are doing, making, or selling, they see it as real
and worthwhile. Then your success and your
prosperity are assured. Whatever you put into

substance along with faith will work out in manifestation in your world. You demonstrate prosperity by an understanding of the prosperity law and by having faith in it. Faithfulness and earnestness in the application of the prosperity law will assure you of success.

If you have faith in outer things, you are building shadows without substance, shadows that cease as soon as your supporting thought is withdrawn from them, forms that will pass away and leave you nothing.

Do not have faith in anything less than God, in anything other than the one Mind, for when your faith is centered there, you are building for eternity. Mind and the ideas of Mind will never pass away. There will never be an end to God. There will never be an end to Truth, which God is. There will never be an end to substance, which God is. Build with the divine substance. Cultivate faith in realities.

We must find a way to connect ideas of substance with ideas of material expression. This is accomplished by faith through prayer according to our decree. We are always decreeing, sometimes consciously, often unconsciously. With every thought and word we are increasing or diminishing the activity of substance. The resulting manifestation conforms to our thought.

Loyalty   When you first begin to think of
                God as everywhere-present sub-
stance, your mind will not always adhere continuously to the idea. You need to develop
certain stabilizing ideas. One of them is continuity or loyalty to Truth. Love sticks to the
thing on which it has set its mind. Nothing so
tends to stabilize and unify all as love. And
nothing is so important as sticking to the ideal
and never giving up the work we have set out
to accomplish.

Perhaps some adverse condition of your own
thought has prevented a full demonstration. Do
not let this swerve you from your loyalty to the
law. You may seem to attain results very slowly.
That is the best reason for sticking closely to
your ideal and not changing your mind. Be
loyal to Principle. The adverse condition will
break up. The true light will come and the invisible substance you have been faithfully affirming will begin to reveal itself to you in all its
fullness of good. It will destroy your fears, stop
your worries, and change your finances.

Going Forward   It is necessary to let go of
                      old thoughts and condi-
tions after they have served their purpose. One
should lay hold of new ideas and create new
conditions to meet one's requirements. We can-

not lay hold of new ideas and make the new conditions until we have made room for them by eliminating the old.

Things are never so bad as you think. Never allow yourself to be burdened with the thought that you are having a hard time. You do not want a soul structure of that kind and should not build it with those thoughts. You are living in a new age. Yesterday is gone forever. Today is here forever. Something grander is now unfolding. Put yourself in line with the progress of thought in the new age and go forward.

Nothing is too great for you to accomplish, nor is anything too trivial for you to handle with perfection and dispatch. The Spirit will guide you in perfect ways, even in the minute details of your life, if you will let it do so. You must will to do its will and trust it in all your ways. It will lead you unfailingly when you follow it.

To give up all anxiety and trust in the Lord does not mean to sit down and do nothing. We are to work as God works. To work with God as a son follows the occupation of his father, we are to form what God has created. The anxious thought must be eliminated. The perfect abandon of the child of nature must be assumed.

Self Study   There is an all-sufficiency of all things. There is a kingdom of abundance of all things. It may be found by those who seek it and are willing to comply with its laws. Whoever you are and whatever your immediate need, you can demonstrate the laws. If your thoughts are confused, become still and know that you are one with the substance and with the law of its manifestation.

To desire is to have fulfillment. If you are obedient to the Spirit and are willing to follow without protest, the way is easy for you. If you question and argue, you will meet many obstructions and your journey will be long and tedious.

Do not give too close study to yourself or your present condition. To dwell in mind upon your seeming limitations only prolongs their stay and makes your progress slow.

Never allow yourself to come under the control of the "I can't" man. He believes in limitations. He wraps his talent in them. He hides it away in the negative earth. No increase is possible to him.

If there is any lack apparent in your world it is because the requirements of the law of manifestation have not been met. This law is based on mind and its operation is through thoughts and words. God gives the increase. It comes by the operation of the law. Our part is to keep the law.

Use your talent. It will expand wonderfully. Talk about it. Praise it. Give God thanks for it. Act as though it were alive. The increase follows.

See what you need as already manifest and as yours. Do not put it off to some uncertain future time.

Money   Prosperity does not mean the same thing to any two persons. Some people think of prosperity as something separate from their spiritual experience. They live in two worlds. It is not a crime to be rich nor a virtue to be poor. Take God into all your affairs. Do all things to the glory of God seven days a week. Be alert in doing whatever comes to you to do. Be cheerful and competent in the doing, sure of the results.

No one is ever given the keys to the Father's storehouse of wealth until he has proved his faith and his reliability. Supply unfolds at the same rate as the need or ability to use substance is developed. The more conscious you become of the presence of the living substance the more it will manifest itself for you and the richer will be the common good of all.

There is an inherent faculty that instinctively lays hold of what it calls its own. The power of the mind to draw to us those things to which we are divinely entitled is a power that can be cultivated, and should be.

Substance in the form of money is given to us for constructive uses. It is given for use and to meet an immediate need, not to be hoarded away or be foolishly wasted.

If you ask for money, do not look for an angel from the skies to bring it on a golden platter. Keep your eyes open for some fresh opportunity to make money. An opportunity will come as sure as you live.

Money is man's instrument, not his master. Money was made for man, not man for money. It is not money that controls men, but the ideas and beliefs they have about money. Every man should be taught how to handle ideas, rather than money, so that they serve him rather than have dominion over him.

You may think that you could live better and do more good if you had lots of money. Things would not be a bit better with you if you had a million dollars, unless you also had the understanding to use it for the good of yourself and others. Would you give a child a million dollars to go buy candy and ice cream for himself? We must evolve with our possessions until we get the ability to handle them. Then the law is fulfilled.

You must have in your finances a consciousness of the permanency of the omnipresent substance as it abides in you. You are standing in the very midst of it. When you take a prosperity thought, hold it. Refuse to be shaken from your spiritual stand in the very midst of God's prosperity and plenty, and supply will begin to come forth and plenty will become more and more manifest in your affairs.

Men's thoughts about money are like their thoughts about all possessions. They believe that things coming out of the earth are theirs to claim and control as personal property. They must give up some of their erroneous beliefs about their "rights." They must learn that they cannot possess and lock up that which belongs to God without themselves suffering the effects of that sequestration.

Every thought of personal possession must be dropped out of mind before men can come into the realization of the invisible supply. They cannot possess money, houses, or lands selfishly, because they cannot possess the universal ideas for which these symbols stand. No man can possess any idea as his own permanently. He may possess its material symbol for a little time on the plane of phenomena. It is the mind that believes in personal possessions that limits the full idea.

Money can indeed be a cheat. It promises

ease and brings cares. It promises pleasures and
pays with pain. It promises influence and returns envy and jealousy. It promises happiness
and gives sorrow. It promises permanence and
then flies away.

Money saved as "an opportunity fund"
brings an increase of good. It is good to have
some money on hand for good uses, such as
hospitality, education, for developing industries
that will contribute to the good of numbers of
people, for the furtherance of spiritual work,
for helping others to build useful and constructive lives, and for many other purposes
and activities. In such conservation of money
one should keep ever in mind the necessity of
a constructive motive back of the action.

Money accumulated for a definite and definitely constructive purpose is quite a different
thing from money hoarded with the fearful
thought of a "rainy day" or a prolonged season
of lack and suffering. Money saved for a "rainy
day" is always used for just that, for fear attracts that which is feared unfailingly.

Do not expect or prepare for adversity of
any kind. To do so is not only to invite it but to
show a doubt of God and all His promises.
Money hoarded from fear as a motive or with
any miserly thought in mind cannot possibly
bring any blessing. When one finds freedom

from the binding thought of hoarding money, he should not go to the opposite extreme of extravagant spending. Money is to be used, not abused. It is good to keep one's obligations paid.

Do not plan to lay up for the future. Let the future take care of itself. To entertain any fears or doubts on that point saps your strength and depletes your spiritual power. Hold steadily to the thought of the omnipresence of universal supply, its perfect equilibrium, and its swift action in filling every apparent vacuum or place of lack.

If you are fearful that you will not be provided with necessities of life for tomorrow, next week, or next year, or for your old age, or that your children will be left in want, deny the thought. Do not allow yourself for a moment to think of something that is outside the realm of all-careful, all-providing good. You know even from your outer experience that the universe is self-sustaining and that its equilibrium is established by law. The same law that sustains all sustains you as a part. Insulate your mind from the destructive thoughts of all those who labor under the belief in hard times. If your associates talk about the financial stringency, affirm all the more persistently your dependence on the abundance of God.

Blessing   God is the source of a mighty
                  stream of substance. You are a
tributary of that stream, a channel of expression. Blessing the substance increases its flow.
If your money supply is low or your purse seems
empty, take it in your hands and bless it. See it
filled with the living substance ready to become
manifest. As you prepare your meals bless the
food with the thought of spiritual substance.
When you dress, bless your garments and realize
that you are being constantly clothed with God's
substance. Do not center your thought on yourself, your interests, your gains or losses. Realize
the universal nature of substance.

Giving   The act of giving complies with
                 the divine law. It involves the
recognition of God as the Giver of all increase;
and unless we have a recognition of the Source
of our supply we have no assurance of continu-
ing in its use.

Let us give as God gives, unreservedly, and
with no thought of return, making no mental
demands for recompense on those who have
received from us. A gift with reservations is not
a gift; it is a bribe. There is no promise of increase unless we give freely. Let go of the gift
entirely. Recognize the universal scope of the
law. Then the gift has a chance to go out and

to come back multiplied. There is no telling how far the blessing may travel before it comes back. It is a beautiful and encouraging fact that the longer it is in returning, the more hands it is passing through and the more hearts it is blessing. All these hands and hearts add something to it in substance. It is increased all the more when it does return.

True giving is the love and generosity of the Spirit-quickened heart responding to the love and generosity of the Father's heart. Without giving the soul shrivels. When giving is practiced the soul expands and becomes Godlike in the grace of liberality and generosity. No restoration to the likeness of God can be complete unless mind, heart, and soul are daily opening out into the large, free, bestowing spirit which so characterizes our God and Father.

In order that the plan of giving may be successful there are several things that must be observed. First there must be a willing mind. Second, the giving must be done in faith. There must be no withholding because the offering seems small. It is not the amount of the offering but the spirit in which it is given that determines its value and power. The results of giving in faith are sure. The law is unfailing in all ages.

A requisite for keeping the law of giving

and receiving is that the offering shall be a just and fair proportion of all that one receives. Wise distribution is closely related to the matter of filling God's treasury.

To whom shall we give and when are questions quite important. There are several truths that may be considered in this connection. Each person finds it necessary to trust his spirit of wisdom to manifest in his own heart. There are no rules or precedents that one can follow in detail. Careful study of the underlying laws of spiritual giving will help one to exercise these divine faculties as they should be exercised.

True spiritual giving rewards with a double joy. One of the blessings is the satisfying knowledge that we are meeting the law and paying our debt of love and justice to the Lord. The other is the joy of sharing the Lord's bounty. Justice comes first: then generosity.

See yourself as the steward of God handing out His inexhaustible supplies. Be happy in your giving. Do not give with any thought that you are bestowing charity. Do all that you can to annul this mental error. The one with the surplus is simply a steward of God and is merely discharging the work of his stewardship. When one asks for divine wisdom and understanding about giving it becomes a joy both to the giver and the recipient.

Tithing   In the Old Testament the tithe or tenth is mentioned as a reasonable and just return to the Lord by way of acknowledging Him as the source of supply. Tithing is the giving of a tenth of one's supply to God and His work. Tithing is a tacit agreement that man is in partnership with God in the conduct of his finances. This leads to confidence and assurance that whatever is done will bring increase of some kind.

Tithing establishes method in giving. It brings into the consciousness a sense of divine order that is manifested in one's outer life and affairs as increased efficiency and greater prosperity. It is the surest way ever found to demonstrate plenty, for it is God's own law and way of giving.

We are living now under larger and fuller blessings from God than man has ever known. It is meet therefore that we give accordingly and remember the law of the tithe. If a tenth was required under the law in olden times, it is certainly no less fitting that we should give it cheerfully now.

The tithe may be a tenth part of one's salary, wage, or allowance, of the net profits of business, or of money received from the sale of goods. It is based on every form of supply, no matter through what channel it may come, for there are many channels through which man is prospered. The tenth should be set apart for the upkeep of some spiritual work or workers. It should be set apart first even before one's personal expenses are taken out, for in the right relation of things God comes first always. Then everything else follows in divine order and falls into its proper place.

The great promise of prosperity is that if men seek God and His righteousness first, then all shall be added unto them. One of the most practical and sensible ways of seeking God's kingdom first is to be a tither, to put God first in finances. It is the promise of God, and the experience of all who have tried it, that all things necessary to their comfort, welfare, and happiness have been added to them in an overflowing measure. Tithing establishes method in giving and brings into the consciousness a sense of order and fitness that will be manifested in one's outer life and affairs as increased efficiency and greater prosperity.

Another blessing that follows the practice of tithing is the continual "letting go" of what one receives, which keeps one's mind open to the good and from covetousness. Making an occasional large gift and then permitting a lapse of time before another is made will not give this lasting benefit, for one's mind channel may in the meantime become clogged with material thoughts of fear, lack, or selfishness.

When a person tithes he is giving continuously, so that no spirit of grasping, no fear, and no thought of limitations get a hold on him. There is nothing that keeps a person's mind so fearless and so free to receive the good constantly coming to him as the practice of tithing. Each day, week, pay day, whenever it is, the tither gives one tenth. When an increase of prosperity comes to him, as come it will and does, his first thought is to give God the thanks and the tenth of the new amount. The free, open mind thus stayed on God is certain to bring forth joy, real satisfaction in living, and true prosperity. Tithing is based on a law that cannot fail.

Debt   A thought of debt will produce debt. So long as you believe in debt you will go into debt and accumulate the burdens that follow that thought. Whoever has not forgiven all men their debts is likely to fall into debt himself.

Debt is a contradiction of the universal equilibrium. There is no such thing as lack of equilibrium in all the universe. Therefore in Spirit and in Truth there is no debt. Men hold on to a thought of debt. This thought is responsible for a great deal of sorrow and hardship.

Debts exist in the mind. In the mind is the proper place to begin liquidating them. These thought entities must be abolished in mind before their outer manifestations will pass away and stay away. Analyze the thought of debt. You will see it involves a thought of lack. We should fill our mind with thoughts of all-sufficiency. Where there is no lack there can be no debts. The way to pay our debts is by filling our mind with the substance of ideas that are the direct opposite of the thoughts of lack that caused the debts.

See substance everywhere and affirm it, not only for yourself but for everyone else. Especially affirm abundance for those whom you have held in the thought of owing you. You will help them pay their debts more easily than if you merely erased their names from your book of accounts receivable. Help pay the other fellow's debts by forgiving him his debts and declaring for him the abundance that is his already in Spirit. The idea of abundance will also bring its fruits into your own life.

Debts are produced by thoughts of lack, impatient desire, and covetousness. When these thoughts are overcome, debts are overcome, forgiven, and paid in full, and we are free.

The way is now open for you to pay your debts. Surrender them to God along with all your doubts and fears. Give Him full dominion in your life and affairs. Give Him your business, your family affairs, your finances, and let Him pay your debts. He is even now doing it. It is His righteous desire to free you from every burden. He is leading you out of the burden of debt, whether of owing or being owed. Love will bring your own to you.

Waste   Any form of waste is a violation of the divine law of conservation. Men and women scatter their energies to the four winds in the effort to satisfy the desires of the flesh and then wonder why they do not demonstrate prosperity. If your substance is going here, there, and everywhere, being spent in riotous thinking and living, how can it accumulate to the point of demonstration? When you overcome your desire for dissipation, then you will begin to accumulate substance that must manifest itself as prosperity according to the law. Do not spend foolishly or save foolishly.

Lack   The only lack is our own lack of appropriation. We must seek the kingdom of God and appropriate it aright before things will be added to us in fullness.

Overcome any leaning in the direction and every belief that you were meant to be poor. Do not hesitate to think that prosperity is for you. Do not feel unworthy. No one is ever hopeless until he is resigned to his imagined fate.

Deny every appearance of failure. Stand by your guns. Think prosperity. Talk prosperity. Affirm supply, support, and success in the very face of question and doubt. Give thanks for plenty in all your affairs. Know for a certainty that your good is now being fulfilled in Spirit, in mind, and in manifestation.

Every time you say "I am a little short of funds," "I haven't as much money as I need," you are putting a limit on the substance in your own consciousness.

It is important to watch your thoughts so that the larger supply may come through your mind and into your affairs. There is no lack of anything anywhere in reality. The only lack is the fear of lack in the mind of man. We do not need to overcome any lack. We must overcome the fear of lack.

Fear of lack led men to speculate in order to accumulate substance and have a lot of it stored up. This caused a still greater fear of lack in other men. The situation grew worse and worse until it became generally believed that we must pile up the material symbols of substance for a possible lack in the future. We must learn to understand the divine law of supply and the original plan, which is that we have each day our daily bread. Anything more than we need for today is a burden. The substance is here all the time, supplying us with every needful thing. Start with the fundamental proposition that there is plenty for you and for me.

Loss   Deny that you can lose anything. Let go of negative thoughts of financial loss or any other kind of loss. Realize that nothing is ever lost in all the universe. There are opportunities everywhere. There always have been opportunities to produce all that you need financially or otherwise.

New ideas come to you from within. Do not think for a moment that you are limited to the beliefs that come from without. Many of those beliefs are outgrown anyway and have outlived their usefulness. That is why we go through periods of change. Old outworn beliefs should be discarded and replaced with new and better ones. We can find new ways of living and new methods of work. We are not confined to the ways and methods of the past.

Paying Bills   The funds to pay all your
                       bills may not suddenly ap-
pear in a lump sum. As you watch and work
and pray, holding yourself in the consciousness
of God's leadership and His abundance, you
will notice your funds beginning to grow "here
a little, there a little," and increasing more and
more rapidly as your faith increases and your
anxious thoughts are stilled.

Do not yield to the temptation of "easy-pay-
ment plans." Any payment that drains your pay
envelope before you receive it is not an easy payment. Do not allow false pride to tempt you to
put on a thousand-dollar front on a hundred-
dollar salary. There may be times when you are
tempted to miss paying a bill in order to indulge a desire for something. This easily leads
one into the habit of putting off paying, which
fastens the incubus of debt on people before
they realize it.

Creditors   Bless your creditors with the
                     thought of abundance as you
begin to accumulate the wherewithal to pay off
your obligations. Keep the faith they had in you
by including them in your prayer for increase.
There is a legitimate commerce that is carried
on by means of what is called credit. It is a con-
venience to be used by those who appreciate its

value and are careful not to abuse it. To do so would be to ruin it. No one should assume an obligation unless he is prepared to meet it promptly and willingly when it comes due.

Never for a moment allow yourself to entertain any scheme for getting the better of your fellows in any trade or bargain. Hold steadily to the law of equity and justice that is working in and through you. Know for a certainty that you are supplied with everything necessary to fulfill all your requirements. Give full value for everything you get. Demand the same for everything you give. Do not try to enforce that demand by human methods. There is a better way. Think of yourself as Spirit working with powerful spiritual forces. Know that the demands of Spirit must and will be met.

Prosperous Home   The first thing to do in making a demonstration of prosperity in the home is to discard all negative thoughts and words. Build a positive thought atmosphere in the home, an atmosphere that is free from fear and filled with love.

The home is the heart of the nation. The heart is the love center. Love is the world's greatest attractive power. The heart of man, or the home that is the heart of the nation, must be aglow with God's love; then it becomes a magnet drawing all good from every direction.

God has amply provided for every home. The provision is in universal substance which responds only to law. Through the application of the law the substance is drawn to us and begins to work for us.

Never make an assertion in the home, no matter how true it may look on the surface, that you would not want to see persist in the home. By talking lack you are making a comfortable place for this unwelcome guest by your fireside, and it will want to stay. Fill the home with thoughts and words of plenty, love, and God's substance, and the unwelcome guest will soon leave.

If your rooms are empty, deny the appearance. Determine that prosperity is manifest in every part of every room. Never think of yourself as poor or needy. Do not talk about hard times or the necessity for strict economy. Even "the walls have ears" and, unfortunately, memories too. Do not think how little you have but how much you have.

Talk plenty. Think plenty. Give thanks for plenty. Enlist all the members of the home in the same work. Make it a game. It's lots of fun. Better than that, it actually works. Every home can be prosperous.

You should never condemn anything in

your home. If you want new articles of furniture or new clothes to take the place of those you now have, do not talk about your present things as old or shabby. Watch your words. See yourself clothed as befits the child of a King. See your house furnished just as pleases your ideal. Plant in the home atmosphere the seed of richness and abundance. It will all come to you. Use the patience, the wisdom, and the assiduity that the farmer employs in planting and cultivating, and your crop will be sure.

Being like Others The delusion that it is necessary to be just like other people, or to have as much as other people have, causes a spirit of anxiety that hinders the exercise of faith in demonstration. Each one unconsciously follows suggestions and furnishes his home with the same sort of things as his neighbors. Here and there are exceptions. Someone expresses his individuality, overcoming mass suggestion and buying furniture he really wants or that is really comfortable and useful. This free, independent spirit has much in its favor in making a prosperity demonstration.

Do not envy the rich. Never condemn those who have money, merely because they have it and you do not. Do not question how they got their money and wonder whether or not they are honest. All that is none of your business. Your business is to get what belongs to you. You do that by thinking about the omnipresent substance of God and how you can lay hold of it through love. Get in touch with God riches in spirit. Lay hold of them by love and you will have sufficient for every day.

Attitudes   Tell me what kind of thoughts you are holding about yourself and your neighbors, and I can tell you just what you may expect in the way of finances and harmony in your home. Are you suspicious of your neighbors? You cannot love and trust in God if you hate and distrust men. Love and hate, or trust and mistrust, simply cannot both be present in your mind at one time. When you are entertaining one, you may be sure the other is absent. Trust other people, and use the power that you accumulate from that act to trust God. There is magic in it. It works wonders. Love and trust are dynamic, vital powers. Are you accusing men of being thieves, and fearing that they are going to take away from you something that is your own? With such a thought generating fear and even terror in your mind and filling your consciousness with darkness, where is there room for the Father's light of protection? Build walls of love and substance around yourself. Send out swift, invisible messengers of love and trust for your protection. They are better guards than policemen or detectives.

Simple Life   The soul wearies of the wear and tear of the artificial world. There is a great difference between the simple life and lack. The two have been as-sociated in the minds of some people. This is the reason they shun the idea of the simple life. Even those who have come into some degree of spiritual understanding sometimes put out of mind all thought of a simple manner of living. They fear that others will think they are failing to demonstrate prosperity.

The simple life does not imply lack and it is not ascetic. The simple life is a state of con-sciousness. It is peace, contentment, and satis-faction in the joy of living and loving. It is at-tained through thinking about God and wor-shiping Him in spirit and in truth.

Success   Success or failure depends upon the attitude of mind active in both those who achieve success and those who fall under the negations of failure. To attain pros-perity, think about prosperity, industry, and efficiency. Fill your mind to overflowing with thoughts of success; realize that the fullness of all good belongs to you by divine right. To this add a feeling of happiness and joy, and you have the recipe for abundant and lasting prosperity and success.

Whoever seeks supply through Spirit and submits his cause to the law of justice and righteousness always succeeds. The reason why men fail to demonstrate the many promises of divine support is that they cling to some selfish or unjust thought. Once the Christ Mind is perceived and obeyed, success follows.

God prospers us when we give the best that is in us and do all things unto Him, acknowledging Him in all our affairs. This is a sure way to success, and when success does come we should realize that it resulted from the work of Spirit in us, because we made ourself a channel through which the Christ Mind could bring its ideas into manifestation. The true Christian never boasts that he is a self-made man, for he well knows that all that he is and has, together with all that he can ever hope to be or to have, is but God finding expression through him.

Praise and Thanksgiving

IN SPIRIT, praise accumulates. In sense consciousness this faculty is called acquisitiveness. It accumulates material things. Praise opens the portal of the mysterious realm called the superconsciousness where thought is impregnated with an uplifting, transcendent quality. Every lofty ideal, all the inspiration that elevates and idealizes in religion, poetry, and art, originates here. It is the kingdom of the true and real in all things.

Praise is the complement of sight and hearing. It is the redemption of weariness. From it issues the Savior of the world. Instead of a supplication, prayer should be a jubilant thanksgiving. This method of prayer quickens the mind miraculously. Like a mighty magnet, it draws out the spiritual qualities that transform the whole man when they are given expression in mind, body, and affairs.

Spirituality   Spirituality (prayer and praise) is one of the foundation faculties of the mind. It is the consciousness that relates man directly to the Father-Mind. It is quickened and enlarged through prayer and through other forms of religious thought and worship. When we pray we look up from within, not because God is off in the sky, but because this spiritual center is in the top of the head and becomes active and our attention is naturally drawn to it.

Prayer   Prayer is natural to man. It should be cultivated in order to round out his character. Prayer is the language of spirituality. When developed, prayer makes man master in the realm of creative ideas. In order to get results from the use of this faculty, right thinking should be observed here as well as elsewhere. To pray, believing that the prayer may or may not be answered at the will of God, is to miss the mark. It is a law of mind that every idea is fulfilled as soon as conceived. This law holds true in the spiritual realm.

In the light of our knowledge of mind action, the law expressed in these words is clear. Moreover, the faith implied is absolutely necessary to the unfailing answer to prayer. If we pray asking for future fulfillment, we form that kind of thought structure in consciousness, and our prayers are always waiting for that future fulfillment which we have idealized.

If we pray thinking that we do not deserve the things for which we ask, these untrue and indefinite thoughts carry themselves out, and we grow to look upon prayer with doubt and suspicion.

God's Will It should not be inferred that the will of Divine Mind is to be set aside in prayer. We are to pray that the will of God enter into us and become a moving factor in our life. The Father does not take our will from us. He gives us the utmost freedom in the exercise of the will faculty. He also imparts an understanding of the law, through the operation of which we can make any condition that we desire.

Aggregation One of the offices of spirituality is to aggregate divine ideas. Through this action man draws absolutely true ideas from the universal Mind. Thus prayer is cumulative. It accumulates spiritual substance, life, intelligence. It accumulates everything necessary to man's highest expression. When we pray in spiritual understanding, this highest realm of man's mind contacts universal, impersonal Mind; the very Mind of God is joined to the mind of man. God answers our prayers in ideas, thoughts, words; these are translated into the outer realms, in time and condition. It is therefore important that we pray with understanding of the law, important that we always give thanks that our prayers have been answered and fulfilled, regardless of appearances.

With understanding and realization of the relation between the idea and the fulfillment of the idea, Jesus quickened the slow processes of nature, and the loaves and fishes were increased quickly. We may not be able to attain at once such speedy operation of the law, but we shall approximate it, and we shall accelerate natural processes as we hold our beliefs nearer to the perfection of the realm of divine ideas.

Response   Praise is closely related to prayer. It is one of the avenues through which spirituality expresses itself. Through an inherent law of mind, we increase whatever we praise. The whole creation responds to praise, and is glad.

Animal trainers pet and reward their charges with delicacies for acts of obedience. Children glow with joy and gladness when they are praised. Even vegetation grows best for those who praise it. We can praise our own abilities, and our very brain cells will expand and increase in capacity and intelligence when we speak words of encouragement and appreciation to them.

Thought Stuff There is an invisible thought-stuff on which the mind acts, making things through the operation of a law not yet fully understood by man. Every thought moves upon this invisible substance in increasing or diminishing degree. When we praise the richness and opulence of our God, this thought-stuff is tremendously increased in our mental atmosphere. It reflects into everything that our mind and our hands touch. When common things are impregnated with our consciousness of divine substance, they are transformed according to our ideals.

Through persistent application of praise, a failing business proposition can be praised into a successful one. Even inanimate things seem to receive the word of praise, responding in orderly obedience when, before, they seemed unmanageable.

A woman used the law on her sewing machine, which she had been affirming to be in bad order. It gave her no trouble afterward. A linotype operator received a certain spiritual treatment given him by a healer at a certain hour, and his linotype, which had been acting badly, immediately fell into harmonious ways. A woman living in a country town had a rag carpet on her parlor floor. She had for years hoped that this carpet might be replaced by a better one. She heard of the law and began praising the old carpet. Greatly to her surprise, inside of two weeks she was given a new carpet from an unexpected source. These are a few simple illustrations of the possibilities latent in praise. Whether the changes were in the inanimate things, or in the individuals dealings with them, does not matter so long as the desired end was attained.

Health and Supply   Turn the power of praise upon whatever you wish to increase. Give thanks that it is now fulfilling your ideal. The faithful law, faithfully observed, will reward you. You can praise yourself from weakness to strength, from ignorance to intelligence, from lack to affluence, from sickness to health. The little lad with a few loaves and fishes furnished the seed that, through prayer and thanksgiving of Jesus, increased sufficiently to feed five thousand people.

All causes that bring about permanent results originate in Spirit. Spirituality, faith, and love are God-given faculties. When we are raised in consciousness to their plane they act naturally under a spiritual law that we may not comprehend. If we make proper connection with Divine Mind in the kingdom of heaven within us, the Father will surely answer our prayers. No good thing will He withhold from us if we comply with the law.

We all need a better understanding of the nature of God if we are to comply with the laws under which He creates. We must begin by knowing that "God is Spirit." Spirit is everywhere—the breath of life and the knowing quality of mind active in and through all. The highest form of prayer is to open our mind and quietly realize that the one omnipresent intelligence knows our thoughts and instantly answers, even before we have audibly expressed our desires.

This being true, we should ask and at the same time give thanks that we have already received. Jesus expressed this idea. When we think or silently speak in the all-potential substance of Spirit, there is always an unfailing effect.

"Always praise the cooking of the cook" is the instruction of the veteran hobo to the novice. Experience has taught the gentlemen of the road that praise and thanks melt the hardest heart and often open the door to amazing hospitality. Tradespeople have found that "Thank you" has commercial value. The prophets of old knew the power of increase inherent in thanksgiving. "Praise ye the Lord" is repeated again and again in the Psalms.

Increase   We increase our vitality by blessing and giving thanks in spirit. To bring about this increase efficiently we must understand the anatomy of the soul and mind centers.

It has been found by experience that a person increases his blessings by being grateful for what he has. Gratitude even on the mental plane is a great magnet. When gratitude is expressed from the spiritual standpoint it is powerfully augmented. The custom of saying grace at the table has its origin in man's attempt to use this power of increase.

A woman who had been left with a large family and no visible means of support related how wonderfully this law had worked in providing food for her children. In her extremity she had asked the advice of one who understood the law, and she had been told to thank

God silently for abundant supply on her table, regardless of appearances. She and her children began doing this, and in a short time the increase of food was so great at times that it astonished them. Her grocer's bill was met promptly and in most marvelous ways the family was supplied with food. Never after that time did they lack.

A simple word of blessing poured out upon that which we have or that which we can conceive as possible for us as sons of the all-providing God will at least begin to release the superabundance of Spirit substance, and we shall have an inner confidence and faith in the providence of our Father.

Jesus warned us not to be anxious about temporal needs but to pray, believing, and to bless and give thanks; then right in the face of seeming insufficiency we should be enabled to demonstrate plenty.

Get Ready   When we commune with the Spirit within and ask for new ideas, they are always forthcoming. When these ideas from within us are recognized, they go to work and come to the surface. Then all the thoughts we have ever had, as well as the thoughts of other people, are added to them and new things are quickly produced. Let us quit depending slavishly on someone else for everything and become producers, for only in that direction lies happiness and success. Let us begin to concentrate on this inner man, this powerful man who produces things, who gets his ideas from a higher-dimensional realm, who brings ideas from a new territory.

What kind of character are you giving to this inner substance by your thoughts? Change your thought and increase your substance in the mind, as Elisha increased the oil for the widow. Get larger receptacles and plenty of them. Even a very small concept of substance may be added to and increased.

The widow had a very small amount of oil, but as the prophet blessed it, it increased until it filled every vessel she could borrow from the neighbors. We should form the habit of blessing everything that we have.

It may seem foolish to some persons that we bless our nickels, dimes, and dollars, but we know that we are setting the law of increase into operation. All substance is one and connected, whether in the visible or the invisible. The mind likes something that is already formed and tangible for a suggestion to take hold of. With this image the mind sets to work to draw like substance from the invisible realm and thus increase what we have in hand.

Elisha used a small amount of oil to produce a great amount of oil. So when we bless our money or other goods, we are complying with the divine law of increase that has been demonstrated many times.

Blessing and Curse   The Israelites set great store in blessing. Rightly understood, a blessing is a great source of inspiration. It lays a firm foundation in the mind. It brings out the good. A curse sees the evil and emphasizes it. A blessing sees only the good and emphasizes only the good. He who uses his mind to curse gets the curse in return, while the mind that blesses receives blessings in return. Blessing imparts the quickening spiritual power that produces growth and increase. It is the power of multiplication.

Praise is the positive pole of life. If you depreciate your life you decrease your consciousness of life. All who have reached heights in things spiritual have been noted for their devotions. Jesus spent whole nights in prayer. He seemed to be asking the Father and thanking Him in almost the same breath on every occasion where He did a great work or expounded a notable truth. Praise is an active principle in our spiritual thoughts and should be given first place in all our thanksgiving.

Love

LOVE, in Divine Mind, is the idea of universal unity. In expression, love is the power that joins and binds in divine harmony the universe and everything in it. Among the faculties of the mind, love is pivotal. Its center of mentation in the body is the cardiac plexus. The physical representative of love is the heart, the office of which is to equalize the circulation of the blood in the body. As the heart equalizes the life flow in the body, so love harmonizes the thought of the mind.

We connect our soul forces with whatever we center our love upon. If we love the things of sense or materiality, we are joined or attached to them through a fixed law of being. In the divine order of being, the soul, or thinking part, of man is joined to its spiritual ego. If it allows itself to become joined to the outer or sense consciousness, it makes personal images that are limitations.

Regeneration   In the regeneration, our love goes through a transformation, which broadens, strengthens, and deepens it. We no longer confine love to family, friends, and personal relations, but expand it to include all things. The denial of human relationships seems at first glance to be a repudiation of the family group, but it is merely a cleansing of the mind from limited beliefs of love when this faculty would satisfy itself solely by means of human kinship.

Meditate on Love   One should make it a practice to meditate regularly on the love idea in universal Mind, with the prayer, *"Divine love, manifest thyself in me."* There should be periods of mental concentration on love. Think about love, and all the ideas that go to make up love will be set into motion. This produces a positive love current which, when sent forth with power, will break up opposing thoughts of hate, and render them null and void.

The thought of hate will be dissolved, not only in the mind of the thinker but in the minds of those with whom he comes in contact in mind or in body.

The love current is not a projection of the will. It is a setting free of a natural, equalizing, harmonizing force that in most persons has been dammed up by human limitations.

The ordinary man is not aware that he possesses this mighty power, which will turn away every shaft of hate that is aimed at him. Here is a faculty native to man, existent in every soul, which may be used at all times to bring about harmony and unity among those who have been disunited through misunderstanding, contentions, or selfishness.

Love is more than mere affection, and all our words protesting our love are not of value unless we have this inner current, which is real substance. Though we have the eloquence of men and of angels, and have not this deeper feeling, it profits us nothing. We should deny the mere conventional, surface affection, and should set our mind on the substance of love.

Phases   Charity is not love. You may be kindhearted, and give to the poor and needy until you are impoverished, yet not acquire love. You may be a martyr to the cause of Truth and consume your vitality in good works, yet be far from love. Love is a force that runs in the mind and body like molten gold in a furnace. It does not mix with the baser metals. It has no affinity for anything less than itself. Love is patient. It never gets weary or discouraged. Love is always kind and gentle. It does not envy. Jealousy has no place in its world. Love never becomes puffed up with human pride, and does not brag about itself. It is love that makes the refinement of the natural gentleman or lady, although he or she may be ignorant of the world's standards of culture. Love does not seek its own. Its own comes to it without being sought.

Jesus came proclaiming the spiritual interrelationship of the human family. His teaching was always of gentleness, nonresistance, love. To do this, one must be established in the consciousness of divine love, and there must be discipline of the mental nature to preserve such a high standard. The divine law is founded in the eternal unity of all things.

Fearlessness Divine love in the heart establishes one in fearlessness and indomitable courage. A woman who understands this law was waylaid by a tramp. She looked him steadily in the eye and said, "God loves you." He released his hold upon her and slunk away. Another woman saw a man beating a horse that could not pull a load up a hill. She silently said to the man, "The love of God fills your heart and you are tender and kind." He unhitched the horse; the grateful animal walked directly over to the house where the woman was, and put his nose against the window behind which she stood. A young girl sang "Jesus, Lover of My Soul" to a calloused criminal; the man's heart was softened, and he was reformed.

The new heaven and the new earth that are now being established among men and nations the world over are based on love. When men understand each other, love increases. This is true not only among men, but between men and the animal world, and even between man and the vegetable world.

Feelings   We may talk about the wisdom of God, but the love of God must be felt in the heart. It cannot be described, and one who has not felt it can have no concept of it from the descriptions of others. The more we talk about love, the stronger it grows in the consciousness. If we persist in thinking loving thoughts and speaking loving words, we are sure to bring into our experience the feeling of that great love that is beyond description—the very love of God.

Purity   It is popularly taught and believed that there is but one love; that God is love and that all love is from Him, hence that all love is God's love. Love is a divine principle and man can know it in its purity by touching it at its fountainhead. There it is not tinged in any way by man's formative thought, but flows forth a pure, pellucid stream of infinite ecstasy. It has no consciousness of good or evil, pure or impure, but pours itself out in great oceans of living magnetic power, to be used by whosoever will.

Thinking gives color, tone, shape, character to all creation. Error thought has put greed into love. Wherever love is tainted with selfishness, we may know that error thought has made muddy its clear stream, so that it no longer represents the purity of its source.

A Magnet   Love is the drawing power of mind. It is the magnet of the universe, and about it may be clustered all the attributes of Being, by one who thinks in divine order. Many who have found the law of true thinking and its effect wonder why supply does not come to them after months and years of holding thoughts of bounty. It is because they have not developed love. They have formed the right image in mind, but the magnet that draws the substance from the storehouse of Being has not been set into action.

To demonstrate supply, we must think supply, and thus form it in the consciousness. We must conserve all the ideas of substance in the mind. We must vibrate with love in thought, word, and act. Then will come to us on the wings of invisibility that which will satisfy every need. This is the secret of demonstrating plenty.

Love never sees anything wrong in that which it loves. If it did, it would not be pure love. Pure love is without discriminating power. It simply pours itself out upon the object of its affection, and takes no account of the result. By so doing, love sometimes casts its pearls before swine, but its power is so great that it transforms all that it touches.

Evil   Do not be afraid to pour out your love upon all the so-called evil in the world. Deny the appearance of evil, and affirm the omnipotence and omnipresence of love and goodness. Take no account of the evil that appears in your life and your affairs. Refuse to see it as evil. Declare that what seems evil has somewhere a good side, which shall through your persistent affirmation of its presence be made visible. By using this creative power of your own thought you will change that which seemed evil into good, and divine love will pour its healing balm over all.

Always remember that love is the great magnet of God. It is, of itself, neither good nor evil. These are qualities given to it by the thinking faculty in man. Whatever you see for your love, that it will draw to you, because as a magnet it attracts whatever you set your desire upon.

To focus your love about self and selfish aims will cause it to draw around you the limited things of personality and the hollow shams of sense life. To focus your love upon money and the possessions of the material world will make you the slave of it, and will make your life a failure and a disappointment.

Difficulties   You may trust love to get you out of your difficulties. There is nothing too hard for it to accomplish for you, if you put your confidence in it and act without dissimulation. Do not talk love and in your heart feel resentment. This will bring discord to your body. Love is candor and frankness. Deception is no part of love. He who tries to use it in that sort of company will prove itself a liar, and love will desert him in the end.

Love is satisfaction in itself—not that satisfaction with personal self, its possessions and its attractions, which is vanity, but an inner satisfaction that sees good everywhere and in everybody. It insists that all is good, and by refusing to see anything but good it causes that quality to appear uppermost in itself and in all things. When only good is seen and felt, how can there be anything but satisfaction?

Universal Goal   When love, the universal magnet, is brought into action in the consciousness of our race, it will change all our methods of supplying human wants. It will harmonize all the forces of nature and will dissolve the discords that now infest earth and air. It will control the elements until they obey man and bring forth that which will supply all his needs without the labor that is called the sweat of his face. The earth shall yet be made paradise by the power of love. That condition will begin to set in for each one just as soon as he develops the love nature in himself.

Forgiveness

FORGIVENESS is a process of giving up the false for the true; erasing sin and error from the mind and body. It is closely related to repentance, which is a turning from belief in sin to belief in God and righteousness. A sin is the falling short of divine law. True forgiveness is only established through renewing of the mind and body with thoughts and words of Truth.

Forgiveness really means the giving up of something you should not do. Jesus said that man has power to forgive sin. Repentance and forgiveness are the only means that man has of getting out of sin and its effect and coming into harmony with the law.

Repentance   Repentance is a reversal of mind and heart in the direction of the All-Good. When we repent, we break with human thought and ascend into a spiritual thought realm, the kingdom of God.

The Greek word *metanoia* is translated "repentance," which has been interpreted to mean an admission to God of sorrow for past sin and a resolve to be good in the future. The field of action for that which has been assumed to be goodness in the sight of God has nearly always been in conduct.

There is always hope for the repentant sinner. A repentant state of mind is an exceeding good state for one who has been on the error side. If you find yourself suffering the result of transgressed law, begin at once a righteous repentance. As soon as you repent and recognize that the way of Spirit is the way of pleasantness, your sins are forgiven you, and you are made whole and well.

Law   The law is Truth. Truth is all that is good. There is no power or no reality in sin. If sin were real and enduring, like goodness and Truth, it could not be forgiven but would hold its victim forever. Our first work in the demonstration is to contact God. Therefore, we must forgive all men their transgressions. Through the divine law of forgiveness we cleanse our mind so that the Father can forgive us.

Man can do everything with the thoughts of his mind. They are absolutely under his control. He can direct them. He can coerce them. He can hush them or crush them. He can dissolve one thought and put another in its stead. There is no other place in the universe where man has mastery. The dominion that is his by divine right is over his own thoughts, only. When man apprehends this and begins to exercise that dominion, he begins to open the way to God— the only door to God—through mind and thought.

Law of Dissolving   How can you expect to forgive your trans-gressions before you have first forgiven others their transgressions? One of the laws of mind is that one belief must be dissolved before another can take its place. If you have in mind a thought that someone has wronged you, you cannot let in the cleansing power of Spirit until you have dissolved and cast out the belief of the wrong.

You may be wondering why you do not get spiritual illumination as others do. What kind of thoughts fill your mind? Have you by forgiving your debtors made room in your life for spiritual blessings, or is your mind filled with thoughts of resentment against this one, and a feeling that you have been slighted by that one? Jesus recognized this infallible law of mind.

Thoughts have substance and form. They may easily be taken to be permanent by one who lacks spiritual discernment. They bring forth fruit according to the seed ideas planted into the mind. They are not enduring unless founded in Spirit.

The question is not "How guilty is that man," but "How do I stand in the sight of the Father as to my ideas about his guilt?" Reform yourself first. That means very much more to one who enjoys an understanding of mind and its laws than it does to the ordinary individual.

He who knows not himself wholly, but just his superficial, external personality, thinks that he is reformed when he conforms to moral and municipal laws. He may be filled with self-righteousness and may daily lift his voice in prayer, thanking God that he is not as other men are; but he has not forgiven men their transgressions. He looks upon every man who does not conform to his understanding of morality, religion, or finances as a transgressor, and thanks God for his own supposed insight and keenness. But he is not at peace. There is something lacking. God does not talk to him "face to face," because the mind, where God and man meet, is darkened by the murky belief that other men are sinners. God is too pure to behold iniquity, so our first work of reform is to forgive all men their transgressions. Through this forgiving act on our part, the Father can enter with forgiveness of our transgressions.

Forgiving All   Our forgiving "all men" includes ourself. You must also forgive yourself. Let the finger of denial erase every sin or "falling short" that you have charged up against yourself. Pay your debt by saying to that part of yourself which you think has fallen short: "See, you are well! sin no more, that nothing worse befall you." Then "loose him, and let him go."

Treat sin as a mental transgression, instead of considering it as a moral defection. Deny in thought all tendency to the error way and hold yourself firmly to the Christ Spirit, which is your divine self. Part company forever with the "accusing conscience." Those who have resolved to sin no more have nothing in common with guilt.

Forgiving Debts   Deny that any man or
                         woman owes you any-
thing. If necessary, go over your list of names
separately and sincerely forgive the thought of
debt which you have been attaching to each person named. More bills may be collected in this
way than in any other, for many of these people will pay what they owe when you send them
this forgiving thought.

Let the law of plenty work itself out in you
and in your affairs. This is the way the Father
forgives your debts: not by canceling them on
His books but by erasing them from His mind.
He remembers them no more against you when
you deny their reality. The Father is the everywhere-present Spirit in which all that appears
has its origin. God's love sees you always well,
happy, and abundantly provided for. God's wisdom demands that order and right relation
exist in your mind before it may become manifest in your affairs as abundance. His love would
give you your every desire, but His wisdom or-
dains that you forgive your debtors before your
debts are forgiven.

To remedy any state of limited finances or
ill health that has been brought about by worry,
one must begin by eliminating the worry that
is the original cause. One must free one's mind
from the burden before the debt can be paid.

Many people have found that the statement
"I owe no man anything but love" has helped
them greatly to counteract this thought of debt.
As they used the words their minds were opened
to an inflow of divine love and they faithfully
cooperated with the divine law of forgiveness
in thought, word, and deed. They built up such
a strong consciousness of the healing and en-
riching power of God's love that they could live
and work peacefully and profitably with their
associates. Thus renewed constantly in health, in
faith, and in integrity, they were able to meet
every obligation that came to them.

The statement *"I owe no man anything but
love"* does not mean that we can disclaim owing
our creditors money or try to evade the payment
of obligations we have incurred. The thing denied is the burdensome thought of debt or of
lack. The work of paying debts is an inner work
having nothing to do with the debts already
owed but with the wrong thoughts that produced them. When one holds to the right ideas,
burdensome debts will not be contracted.

Love   Your thoughts should at all times be
            worthy of your highest self, your
fellow man, and God. The thoughts that most
frequently work ill to you and your associates
are thoughts of criticism and condemnation. Fill

your mind with thoughts of divine love, justice, peace, and forgiveness. This will pay your debts of love, which are the only debts you really owe. Then see how quickly and easily and naturally all your outer debts will be paid and all inharmonies of mind, body, and affairs will smooth out at the same time. Nothing will so quickly enrich your mind and free it from every thought of lack as the realization of divine love. Divine love will free you quickly and perfectly from the burden of debt and heal you of your physical infirmities, often caused by depression, worry, and financial fear. Love will bring your own to you. Adjust all misunderstandings and make your life and affairs healthy, happy, harmonious, and free, as they should be. Love indeed is the "fulfilling of the law."

In the kingdom of Truth and reality, ideas are the coin of the realm. You can use the new ideas that divine wisdom is now quickening in your mind and start this very moment to pay your debts.

Freedom   Begin by thanking God for your freedom from debt-burden thought. This is an important step in breaking the shackles of debt. Debt is soon vanquished when wisdom and good judgment are in control.

Begin to free yourself at once by doing all that is possible with the means you have and as you proceed in this spirit the way will open for you to do more; for through the avenues of Spirit more means will come to you and every obligation will be met.

No one can understand how forgiveness sets free the sin-bound soul and the sick body unless he studies mind and has some understanding of its laws. There is a universal thought substance in which thought builds whatever man wills.

Change   There must be inner growth that is a fuller consciousness of the new life which comes with the entering into the kingdom of Christ. There is a foundation for a worldwide movement in behalf of purer men and better things for all. There is something back of it all, and the old conditions, diseases, and limitations must pass away. The time is now ripe for entering into this kingdom, this attainment of the spiritual side of life, this growing of a new body; and every one of us can enter in if only we will do so.

In all actual transformation of mind and body a dissolving, breaking-up process necessarily takes place, because thought force and substance have been built into the errors that appear. In each individual these errors have the power that man has given them by his thought concerning them. These thought structures must be broken up and eliminated from consciousness.

The simplest, most direct, and most effective method is to withdraw from them the life and substance that have been going to feed them, and to let them shrivel away into their own nothingness. This withdrawal is best accomplished by denial and forgiveness of the power and reality of evil and the affirmation of the allness of Spirit.

Nothing is destroyed, because "nothing cannot be destroyed. The change that takes place is merely a transference of power from an error belief to faith in the Truth, through the recognition that God is good and is all that in reality exists.

To get the actual overcoming power of Christ we must appreciate life and enter into it thankfully and heartily. The abundant life is always present. When we recognize it and open our consciousness to it, it comes flowing into mind and body with a mighty quickening, healing power that renews, transforms, and changes.

Adam and Eve

THE BIBLE veils in its history the march of man from innocence and ignorance to a measure of sophistication and understanding. Over all hovers the divine idea of man, the perfect-man pattern, the Lord, who is a perpetual source of inspiration and power for every man.

Allegory   What is stated in the Book of Genesis in the form of allegory can be reduced to ideas. These ideas can be worked out by the guidance of mental laws.

God creates through the action of His mind, and all things rest on ideas. Divine Mind images its ideas definitely and in every detail. The idea precedes the fulfillment. Ideas are productive and bring forth after their kind. They express themselves under the law of divine imagery.

The Book of Genesis gives two accounts of the creation of man; the first is that of the creation by Elohim and the second is that of the creation by Jehovah. The first act of mind is the formation of the idea, and the second is the expression of that idea. Elohim or God-Mind creates a Spiritual Man, in whom are conceived to be present all the attributes of his source. Next this Spiritual Man, Jehovah God, God-Mind identified as I AM, forms man in spiritual substance, in the "dust of the ground."

Adam   Adam is the first movement of mind in its contact with life and substance. He represents the generic man, or the whole human race epitomized in an individual-man idea.

If the ego, or will, which is man, has adhered to wisdom faithfully and has carried out in its work the plans that are idealized in wisdom, it has created a harmonious consciousness. Adam in the Garden of Eden is symbolical of that consciousness.

Eve   Eve is love, or feeling, in individual consciousness. The I AM (wisdom) puts feeling into what it thinks, and so Eve (feeling) becomes the "mother of all living." Feeling is Spirit which quickens. Woman symbolizes the soul region of man and is the mother principle of God in expression. Back of the woman (feeling) is the pure life essence of God.

Eden   Eden is a pleasant, harmonious, productive state of consciousness in which are all possibilities of growth. When man is expressing in harmony with Divine Mind, bringing forth the qualities of Being in divine order, he dwells in Eden, or in a state of bliss in a harmonious body.

The "garden" symbolizes the spiritual body in which man dwells when he brings forth his thoughts after the original divine ideas. This garden is the substance of God or state of perfect relation of ideas to Being. The Garden of Eden is the divine consciousness.

The Fall   Adam in his original creation was in spiritual illumination. Spirit breathed into him continually the necessary inspiration and knowledge to give him superior understanding. But he began eating,

or appropriating, beliefs in two powers—God
and not-God, or good and evil. The result, so
the allegory relates, was that he fell away from
spiritual life and all that it involves.

Having developed a consciousness apart
from his divine nature, man must "till the
ground from which he was taken," that is, he
must come into a realization of God as the
source of his Being and must express ideas in
harmony with Divine Mind.

Adamic Consciousness

Man is Spirit, ab-
solute and uncon-
ditioned; but man forms an Adamic consciousness into which he breathes the breath of life;
this, in its perfect expression, is the Son of man,
and expression of the divine idea. This Adam
is all of what we term soul, intellect, and body.
We are continually at work with this Adam. We
can breathe into his nostrils the breath of life,
inspiring him with the idea of life in all its unlimited fullness. We can lift up this Adam by
infusing into him these sublime ideas, and in
no other way. Wisdom and love are joined in
God, and a perfect balance is struck in consciousness between knowing and feeling when
man spiritualizes his thoughts.

Man is falling just to the extent that he is
ignoring the living Word in himself. Man must

keep affirming the living Word; then he will have the transformed body. Jesus Christ is the Word demonstrated as perfect man, and through Him we are saved from the fall.

Development　　Time is a human invention and acts as a barrier to a broader conception of creative processes. All attempts to find a date for the beginning of man are futile. Years are associated with events, and when the events are past the years go with them. States of mind make events, and new states of mind are constantly being formed; consequently every moment is the beginning of a new creation to the individual. It is of no practical value to a man to know that the world has journeyed around the sun six thousand or six million years since it was formed. The important thing is to know where man stands in relation to the creative law.

The Bible puts history before us as if we were part of every event, which we are. The one Mind is moving in its realm of ideas "over all, and through all, and in all."

The allegory of the Garden of Eden, of the man and the woman and the serpent, represents the development of ideas in individual consciousness, not the development of a planetary system. Creation is the evolution of ideas in mind. Creation is the development of individuality; hence the one object of all creative processes is the making of man.

In the development of individuality the factors described in the allegory are active in every one of us at this moment. The creating is going on right now. The reason why God created man potentially perfect and then set him the task of proving it is found in the mysterious process called self-identification. Man makes himself after the pattern designed by the Great Architect. In proving his ability to carry out the divine plan he proves himself perfect.

The Serpent   Three fundamental factors are at the basis of all manifestation, namely intelligence, life, and substance. Divine intelligence reveals perfect ideas as the basis of existence. Any conception other than this is "eating" or appropriating thoughts that seem both good and evil. This conception of opposites leads to all kinds of inharmonies. It is the serpent, "more subtle than any other wild creature," that suggests this to man. The serpent represents life, in which is vibration, color, sound, in fact all sensation. Sense consciousness is another name for the serpent. The life idea is manifest in the mighty lightning chain darting from sky to earth as well as in the subtle sensations that sweep through the soul.

Indulgence   The soul (Eve) is attracted by this realm of sensation and is psychologized by its promises of pleasure. When we indulge any of the sensations of the flesh for the mere pleasure that accompanies the indulgence, we are following the delusive suggestions of the serpent instead of listening to the word of God. Pain, disease, and finally death always result from such ignorant transgression of the divine law. Life is a fundamental factor in all existence. Without life there could be no existence.

When man fails to master his sensations and gives himself up to the uncontrolled enjoyment of life, he is losing his dominion and must suffer the consequences of transgressing the law. Man should therefore be ever on the alert to maintain his dominion and mastery over all the ideas of the mind and sensations of the body. Everything has its use in the divine economy, and man as the master builder should ever be seeking to carry out the divine plan.

Wisdom   Wisdom shows us what the law is and where we have fallen short in our use of it. We are not punished for our sins but by them. We establish ruling attitudes of mind by our daily thoughts. They may or may not be in harmony with Principle. Our dominant thoughts establish a general character. What we love or what we hate builds cells of joy or pain.

Obedience   To be in subjection to the higher Power is the highest goal of human attainment. The spirit of obedience is the spirit of love. Love is the most obedient thing in the universe. It is also the greatest worker and will accomplish more for our happiness than all other faculties combined. Love is divine ordinance. It has a balm for every ill.

Disobedience to Spirit is refusal to do right at all hazards. We all know the right. We do not always do it, because it seems to foil immediate attainment of the objective that we seek. We want quick returns.

If you are obedient to Spirit you will not suffer burdens. You will live in the present, do your highest duty every day, forget the past, and let the future take care of itself. To trust Spirit you must know of its guidance by experience.

Conscience

THERE is a divine goodness at the root of all existence. It is not necessary to give in detail the place of abode of each sentient part of this central goodness, for it is there, wherever you look, and whenever you look. No man is so lowly but that at the touch of its secret this divine goodness may be brought to light in him. Even the animals exhibit its regulating and directive power. This goodness sleeps in the recesses of every mind and comes forth when least expected.

Many stifle it for years, maybe for ages, but eventually its day comes, and there is a day of

reckoning. This is the law of universal balance
—the equilibrium of Being. It cannot be put
aside with transcendental philosophies or metaphysical denials any more than it can be smoth-
ered in the forces of the blind passions.

Monitor   Men and women are loath to ad-
                   mit that there is within them a
monitor with which they have sooner or later
to cope. They put off the day of reckoning as
long as possible. They do not like to deal with
this leveler of Spirit. It is too exact. It wants
justice to the very limit.

Whoever has felt the prick of conscience
has been spoken to by the Holy Spirit. Whoever
has sat at the feet of his own inner conviction
has been aware of God's presence.

Guidance   Man is never without a guide,
                   no matter how loudly he may
be crying out for leading. There is always at
hand a sure torchbearer if he will but follow
the light. It is too simple, too easy! Man has
formed in his mind a far-off God who talks to
him from some high mountain in invisible
space. By thus looking afar for his God he
ignores the spark of divinity shining in his own
being.

Herein is man fooled into believing that he

can do the things that are not in harmony with his ideas of goodness and yet escape the consequences. He presumes that God is too far away to behold his shortcomings. He loses sight of the fact that God is right with him every moment.

This is the meaning of the old saying that a man and his conscience are good friends as long as the way is smooth. When it grows rugged, they fall out. They fall out because man has reached a point where he begins to consider his ways and he looks carefully over the life he is leading. This brings him to a beholding state of mind. He sees that what he considered right in the clear light of divine good is not up to standard. Here the divergence takes place between man and his conscience. They were friends in appearance only before or during the period of license. The conscience may seem to assent to the derelictions of man, but it is ever the inner protestant that keeps knocking at the consciousness until the steps are arrested.

Questionable Methods

Worldly fortune is not always a blessing to man. In fact, under present customs it is apt to be just the reverse. As long as questionable methods are successful in bringing results, conscience has but a small chance for a hearing. It is only when failure follows the efforts of the misguided that conscience gets his ear. Then the field is surveyed with the eye of a general defeated in an unjust cause. The heat of battle blinded him, and he gave no thought to the lives he was uselessly sacrificing.

Here remorse gnaws the vitals of the unwise. Here the true wisdom is revealed. It is said that experience is a dear school, and only the wise learn therein. This carries with it its own nullification, like many of the intellect's wise observations. Experience is the school of fools. The truly wise do not take lessons within her doors.

Understanding   There are two ways to get understanding. One is to follow the guidance of the Spirit that dwells within, and the other is to go blindly ahead and learn by hard experience. These two ways are open to everyone. It is recognized by the man who has had experience that he can advise the one who has not and thus save him the laborious steps of that rocky road. In the light of omnipresent intelligence, is there not One who knows all things, all roads, all combinations, and what will be the outcome of every one?

Prophecy   Do not men and women by their constant efforts to peer into the future prophesy a wisdom that knows all future? They certainly do. When man looks in the right direction he finds such an oracle.

It is the prerogative of Spirit to know the future. When man consults Spirit with pure heart and unselfish motives he has pointed out to him the very lines his life shall be cast in if he is obedient to his most high God.

It is no great achievement for one who follows the leading of Spirit within to forecast the future. To Spirit the future is a succession of events based on the ideas revolving in the mind at present. Whoever rides into his own ideal realm can read his future for himself. He finds there a chain of causes at work that he can easily see will produce certain results. It is not necessary for him to read the definite line along which each separate idea will travel to its ultimate. This is the method of reasoning from cause to effect. In Spirit, cause and effect are one. They appear as one and the ultimate is just as clear as the inception.

In mind, all things reach fruition the very instant they are conceived. Time not being a factor, how can there be a beginning and an ending? The architect plans a house and sees it finished in his mind before a single stone is laid or a pound of earth excavated. He can change his plan many times before the con-

struction commences. He can destroy it entirely
if he so desires. So man builds the house of his
own conscience. If he has been planning to
build a home for himself alone, in which there
is but one room, he created in mind just such a
plan, and it is complete and awaits its coming
into visibility. If he has made a plan of a larger
structure, in which are many rooms, this plan
will also come into visibility.

Wasteful Speech   Some persons build their
                         houses far ahead in mind
and say nothing to anyone. Such persons make
very substantial plans, which are infused with
the most enduring substance of the invisible.

Talking is a waste of energy—a dissipater of
power. If you want the greatest success, do not
talk too much about your plans. Keep a reserve
force of new ideas always on hand as a generative center. Let your work speak for itself.

Dynamics   The electrician recognizes a
                  certain universal law of action
in the revolutions he builds into his dynamo.
The energy produced is based on the size and
texture of the dynamo and the rapidity of its
motion. Mind has a law of dynamics equally as
scientific. The character of an idea is the estimate of its size. One's active faith in it deter-

mines the rapidity of its motion. Ideas generate energy with a swiftness unparalleled in physical dynamics. Rather than moving inanimate things, they move men and women. Rather than temporarily lighting our streets for a few hours, they light the lamps of intelligence that burn eternally.

The secret of doing this successfully lies in knowing how to handle our ideas. The electrician constantly improves the efficiency of electricity by studying the machinery that generates the power. The same rule holds good in mental dynamics. We must study ideas if we want to improve the service of our body, of our intelligence, and of our surroundings. From ideas flow forth the currents that move the machinery of all of them. If our beliefs are based on Truth and we are satisfied that they will stand the test of the most rigid justice, we do not want to let the currents they produce in our mind leak away on some grounded wire.

The world is full of people who are filled with high and mighty resolves to do good. They are sincere, but they are connected with grounded wires. We must keep our wires properly insulated, or our plant will not prove successful.

For instance, we are holding an idea of health, which is generating currents in our mind that might flow out on the wires of faith and heal the world. But we have broken the current by believing that it should pass through a pill, a magnetic hand, or the mind of someone who we think is stronger than we are. We must stop all this and send our idea of health straight to the mark on the wires of our own true word. We have an intuitively correct idea of the truth on every question that comes to our mind, but we do not trust the idea. We impede its free currents by believing that some book, some person, or some church organization has sifted the truth and somehow established it before we came into existence. This fallacy makes a menial of the genius and puts out the light of the world in the minds of generation after generation of the sons of God.

Spiritual ideas must have spiritual wires, or their power dissipates. So we need to watch both the beliefs we hold and the words with which we set them free. If we have an ideal world in which we see things as we want them, yet think it an impossibility that that world may be realized here and now, we are dissipating the power that our ideas are generating. So throughout the category of thought generation, every idea must have a wire that corresponds to its circuit or current. Our words, our acts, and our whole life must be in accord with our ideas.

Available Ideas   The realm of ideas is at
the call of each of us. It
is, in fact, the source from which we draw our
real sustenance. It exists in Being as universal
intelligence. Since it is the cause and source of
all intelligence, sooner or later it must assert its
unobstructed sway in the life of all mankind.
When this realm of ideas becomes so active in
the consciousness that it attracts our special attention, we call it a quickening conscience. It
is the universal intelligence of Being asserting
its inherent moral equilibriums. Man cannot always distort the fair face of the God-Image,
whose likeness he is. He may for a season wear
the grotesque mask of the mountebank or the
fool, but in God's own good time he will be
unmasked by the silent inner self that must be
heard when its hour has come. God is not
mocked, nor is the secret place of the Most
High in every heart forever made a cave for
thieves.

Listening   When conscience cries out in
your heart, "Make straight the
way of the Lord," you will save time by heeding
it. Let its cleansing waters of denial flow over
you. Change your beliefs. Be meek and lowly.
Let your thoughts go up to the Christ Spirit.
Acknowledge Him as One whom you, in your

human consciousness, are not able to comprehend in the majesty of His spiritual understanding.

If you are of a haughty, domineering, self-sufficient will, you stand as Herod, the ruler of Judea. You are married to the passions of the human soul. These passions lead you into sense gratifications so deep, so degrading that you cut off the head of conscience that would have turned you into the highway of good. But the reign of the sense man is shortlived. Your kingdom is taken from you, and you are banished from your native land. This was the fate of Herod after he beheaded John the Baptist. This is the fate of everyone who refuses to listen to the voice of his higher self.

Meekness   The key to the development of Jesus' great powers was in His meek and lowly submission to the Father. Whoever makes himself nothing in the presence of God may be possessor of all things below God.

Man is open to God when he wills to be open. This opening is made by our attitude of absolute mental humility in the contemplation of spiritual realities. Thus, the likeness takes on the express image of the Father, and in no other way can it be done.

"I am gentle and lowly in heart," said the

mighty Nazarene. "Not as I will, but as thou wilt," was the mental attitude He always took when communing with the Father. It was always in the same spirit of love and willing obedience to the guidance of a wisdom that He knew transcended His own.

Jesus did not take the universe on His shoulders by affirming His self-sufficiency. He unloaded every burden and rested in the all-sufficiency of the Father. "I can do nothing on my own authority"; "the Father abiding in me doeth his works." This is the total denial of self—the giving up of all personal desires, claims, and aims. Before man can do this successfully he must change his beliefs—there must be a mental house cleaning.

Denial The command, "If any man would come after me, let him deny himself . . . and follow me," is not broadly interpreted by the world. Some men think that self is denied sufficiently when they acknowledge God as mind, life, love, substance, and all else as error; others think that they have only to give up the recognized sins of the world and believe in a personal Savior, Jesus. But the denial of self goes deeper than all this. To be effective, it must reach the very depths of the consciousness and dissolve all the organic forms that the beliefs held by the personal self have there precipitated. Every human body has its stratified layers of consciousness. These strata have, like the earth, been built up layer after layer through ages and ages of sidereal time.

The body we live in is the result of a labor that we began millions of years ago. It is the stored-up memories of our experience in thought generation. We may have dissolved that body ten millions of times, but no part of its reality has ever been lost to us. Because we have failed to energize it to the perpetuation of its form indefinitely is no argument against its being the very body we have had for aeons upon aeons. The form of it changes, but the mental pictures we have formed in all those ages are intact somewhere in our own private gallery.

Selflessness   Now the clouds are clearing
                        away from our world. The
"sun of righteousness" is rising with "healing in its wings." We are awakening to our powers and possibilities as sons of the Most High.

The day of selflessness has come. This day delivers us from all our burdens. We find that we do not have to bear any of the cares of existence on our shoulders. We say with Jesus, "All things have been delivered to me by my Father." We do not breathe for ourself, but rather God breathes in and through us. We do not have a life of our own, but we feel the life of God surging through all our organs. We say to every part of our body, "You are now one with God; you are perfect in His sight."

We do not think and speak by ourself alone. We think and speak God's thoughts after Him, which rush through our mind like a mighty wind. Then tongues of fire come upon us, because we are inspired by the Holy Spirit. Neither do we have possessions of our own nor cares nor troubles about our life or our family. We leave all these things to God. We are absolutely without responsibility when we have fully denied ourself and followed the Christ. All responsibility drops from us when we let go of the belief that we are a personal being, and possessed of parts, passions, and faculties that belong to us personally. Nothing like a personal man exists in the idea of God.

The idea of God is Jesus Christ—one universal man. Men are but the mind organs of that one man. They do not possess of themselves anything whatever, but all that the Christ possesses flows through their consciousness when they have ceased to believe in personality. This is the at-one-ment and the apprehension of that at-one-ment dissolves forever the inner monitor called accusing conscience.

Judgment and Justice

TRUTH is ready at all times to give judgment and justice. As God is love, so God is justice. These qualities are in Divine Mind in unity, but are made manifest in man's consciousness too often in diversity. It is through the Christ Mind in the heart that they are unified. When justice and love meet at the heart center, there are balance, poise, and righteousness. When judgment is divorced from love, and works from the head alone, there goes forth the human cry for justice. In his mere human judgment, man is hard and heartless; he deals out punishment without consideration of motive or cause, and justice goes awry.

Good Judgment   Good judgment is developed from Principle. In its perfection it is expressed through man's mind, with all its absolute relations uncurtailed. Man has the right concept of judgment, and ideally the judges of our courts have that unbiased and unprejudiced discrimination which ever exists in the Absolute. A prejudiced judge is abhorred. A judge who allows himself to be moved by his sympathies is not considered safe.

It is necessary to place judgment in the Absolute in order to demonstrate its supreme power. This is accomplished by one's first declaring that one's judgment is spiritual and not material; that its origin is in God; that all its conclusions are based on Truth and that they are absolutely free from prejudice, false sympathy, or personal ignorance. This gives a working center from which the ego, or I AM, begins to set in order its own thought world. The habit of judging others, even in the most insignificant matters of daily life, must be discontinued. The law of judgment works out in a multitude of directions. If we do not observe it in small things, we shall find ourselves failing in large.

Condemnation   Judging from the plane of the personal leads into condemnation. Condemnation is always followed by the fixing of a penalty. We see faults in others, and pass judgment upon them without considering motives or circumstances. Our judgment is often biased and prejudiced; yet we do not hesitate to think of some form of punishment to be meted out to the guilty one. He may be guilty or not guilty; decision as to his guilt or innocence rests in the divine law. We have no right to pass judgment. In our ignorance we are creating thought forces that will react upon us.

Whatever thought you send out will come back to you. This is an unchangeable law of thought action. A man may be just in all his dealings, yet if he condemns others for their injustice, that thought action will bring him into unjust conditions; so it is not safe to judge except in the Absolute. This is the stand which everyone must take—resting judgment of others in the Absolute. When this is done the tendency to condemn will grow less and less, until man, seeing his fellow man as God sees him, will leave him to the Absolute in all cases where he seems unjust.

Judgment Day   The great judgment day of Scripture indicates a time of separation between the true and the false. There is no warrant for the belief that

God sends man to everlasting punishment. Modern interpreters of the Scripture say that the "hell of fire" referred to by Jesus means simply a state in which purification takes place.

The word "hell" is not translated with clearness sufficient to represent the various meanings of the word in the original language. There are three words from which "hell" is derived: Sheol, "the unseen state"; Hades, "the unseen world"; and Gehenna, "Valley of Hinnom." These are used in various relations, nearly all of them allegorical. Hell is a figure of speech that represents a corrective state of mind. When error has reached its limit, the retroactive law asserts itself, and judgment, being part of that law, brings the penalty upon the transgressor. This penalty is not punishment, but discipline, and if the transgressor is truly repentant and obedient, he is forgiven in Truth.

Vacillation   Another form of thought related to judgment is the vacillating of the mind that never seems to know definitely what is the proper thing to do. There must be singleness of mind and loyalty to true ideas. Everyone should have definite beliefs of what is just and right, and stand by them. Condemnation in any of its forms retards freedom of action in the discriminative faculty. We hold ourselves in guilt and condemnation, the natural energies of the mind are weakened and the whole body become inert.

Unjust Treatment   The remedy for all that appears unjust is denial of condemnation of others, or of self, and affirmation of the great universal Spirit of justice, through which all unequal and unrighteous conditions are finally adjusted.

Observing the conditions that exist in the world, the just man would have them righted according to what he perceives to be the equitable law. Unless such a one has spiritual understanding, he is very likely to bring upon himself physical disabilities in his efforts to reform men. If his feelings come to a point of "righteous indignation," and he "boils" with anger over the evils of the world, he will cook the corpuscles of his blood.

Put all the burdens of the world upon the one supreme Judge and hold every man, and all the conditions in which men are involved, amenable to the law of God. By so doing, you will set into action mind forces powerful and far-reaching.

If you think that you are unjustly treated by your friends, your employers, your government, or those with whom you do business, simply declare the activity of the almighty Mind, and you will set into action mental forces that will find expression in the executors of the law. This is the most lasting reform to which man can apply himself. It is much more effective than legislation or any attempt to control unjust men by human ways.

Jealousy   Jealousy is a form of mental bias that blinds the judgment and causes one to act without weighing the consequences. The remedy for all this is a dismissal of that poor judgment which causes one to be jealous and a fuller trust in the great all-adjusting justice of God.

Success   Success in the world is largely dependent on good judgment. Everywhere businessmen are looking for people who have judgment equal to the making of quick decisions, on the spur of the moment.

By clearing your understanding and acknowledging the one supreme Mind in which is all discrimination, you can cultivate the ability of your mind to arrive quickly at right conclusions. Take the stand that it is your inheritance from God to judge wisely and quickly. Do not depart therefrom by statements of inefficiency in matters of judgment.

When you are in doubt as to the right thing to do in attaining justice in worldly affairs, ask that the eternal Spirit of justice shall go forth in your behalf and bring about and restore to you that which is your very own. Do not ask for anything but your very own under the righteous law. Some people unconsciously overreach in their desire for possessions. When they put the matter into the care of Spirit, and things do not turn out just as they had expected in their self-seeking way, they are disappointed and rebellious. This will not do under the spiritual law, which requires that man shall be satisfied with justice and accept the results, whatever they may be. Justice can be cooperated with by one who believes in things spiritual and he will thereby be made prosperous and happy.

Jesus Christ

JESUS was the Man of Nazareth, son of Mary. According to present-day belief He is the Savior of mankind. Metaphysically He is the I AM in man, the self, the directive power, raised to divine understanding and power—the I AM identity.

His Mission   As the result of lack of conscious connection between the thinking faculty and the fountainhead of existence, humanity had reached a very low state. Then came Jesus of Nazareth, whose mission was to connect the thinker with the true Source of thought. Thinking at random had brought man into a deplorable condition, and his salvation depended on his again joining his consciousness to the Christ. Only through that connection could he be brought back into his Edenic state.

It is plain to any reasonable, unprejudiced mind that Jesus of Nazareth was a religious reformer with a mission from on high. He had an insight into those things which are ever mysteries to men immersed in the sense consciousness. Through His knowledge, and in harmony with His mission, He set into motion spiritual ideas that ever since His ministry have been operative in the world.

It is evident to even a cursory reader of His life and teachings that He was the representative of a thoroughly organized plan to help men into a higher realization of God and their relation to Him.

Jesus Knew   Jesus was keenly conscious of the character of God and His own relationship to Him. He knew God as unlimited love and as ever-present, abundant life. He knew God as wisdom and supply. He knew Him as Father, ever ready and willing to supply every need of the human heart.

Jesus knew that as Son of God He had access to every blessing, to all the wisdom, love, and help of the Father-Mind. He did not simply believe that the words He spoke were true, He *knew* that they were true. His words were pregnant with meaning. They were vital, living words, which carried conviction and which produced immediate results.

Jesus is the Way-Shower. He came that we might have life more abundantly. He came to awaken man to the possibilities of his own nature. He came to bear witness to Truth. He used the one true way to the realization of eternal life and the universal consciousness, therefore His influence on the race cannot be measured. It is infinite and eternal.

Crucifixion   The Jews were under the dominion of an earth-minded priesthood. They were in a state of ignorance as regards spiritual things and did no thinking for themselves. They could not recognize or comprehend the things of which Jesus spoke to them. They were looking for a temporal king who would restore to them, by war and conquest, the earthly glory of Solomon. When Jesus tried to teach them of Spirit, of a spiritual idea, the Christ within themselves that would free them from every bondage of mind, body, and environment, they crucified Him.

Crucifixion is the crossing out in conscious-

ness of errors that have become fixed states of
mind. It is the surrender or death of the whole
personality in order that the Christ Mind may
be expressed in all its fullness.

The crucifixion of Jesus represents the wiping of personality out of consciousness. We
deny the human self so that we may unite with
the selfless. We give up the human so that we
may attain the immortal. We dissolve the
thought of the physical body so that we may
realize the spiritual body.

The Cross represents that state of consciousness termed "mortal mind." The Cross is not
a burden as commonly understood, but a symbol
of the forces in man adjusted in their right
relation.

Jesus Christ   Christ is the perfect idea of
                    God for man. Jesus is the
perfect expression of the divine idea Man. Jesus
Christ is a union of the two, the idea and the
expression, or in other words, He is the perfect
man demonstrated.

Church of Christ   The true Christ church
                       is not an outer sect or
religious denomination. First of all it is an aggregation of spiritual ideas in individual consciousness. To establish the church, or *ecclesia*,

of God in man, a new state of consciousness must be formed. Man must gain an understanding of God as Spirit, and also he must understand his own relation to Spirit.

The church of God begins its activity in man as a mental perception, which must go through certain processes before it is established in the whole consciousness. Its work is subjective first.

In its outer sense the church of Christ consists of all persons in whom the consciousness of Truth has become firmly established; whether or not they belong to a denominational church makes no difference. They comprise that great brotherhood which Jesus Christ established in Spirit.

The true church is not made of creeds and forms. It is not contained in walls of wood and stone. The heart of man is its temple and the Spirit of truth is the one guide into all Truth. When men learn to turn within to the Spirit of truth, who is in each one for his light and inspiration, the differences between the churches of man will be eliminated, and the one church will be recognized.

When the true church is revealed to man's soul, all illusion is dissolved. Man finds that the church of Jesus Christ has to do with the world right here and now. It is not a religion, as he has been accustomed to regard religion. It is an organic principle in nature working along definite lines of growth in the building up of a state of consciousness for the whole human race.

The church of Jesus Christ is an exact science. It has its part in the economy of Being, as the organizer of the unorganized. It does not refer to things abstract, but to things concrete. Whoever looks upon it as an abstraction has wholly misconceived it.

The church of Christ covers every department of man's existence and enters into every fiber of his being. He carries it with him day and night, seven days of the week. He lives in it as a fish lives in water. He becomes conscious of its enveloping presence and is transformed into a new creature. Life becomes an ecstasy and his cup is full to overflowing.

The burdens of the human drop out of sight just as fast as the organic church is constructed. The construction of this church is orderly, definite, and exact. It is not done in a moment, but little by little the man is built from the within to the without, a new creature in consciousness and in body.

The Kingdom
of Jesus Christ

A KINGDOM is a government with evidence of its power right among its subjects. Its authority is exercised in the country in which it is set up. It regulates the public affairs of the people in its domain, to conform to its highest ideas of equity, prosperity, and the general welfare of its subjects.

This was Jesus Christ's idea of a kingdom. His kingdom was not of this world of sin, sickness, poverty, injustice, and death, but a kingdom in which righteousness, health, life, peace, and prosperity are natural to all its people. He proposed to establish such a kingdom among men, through the evidences of His power. Thus were the instructions given to His disciples whom He sent forth as His agents to inaugurate the new order of things.

Kingdom Likenesses

Had the kingdom to which Jesus so often referred been a city with golden streets, in the skies, He could easily have located it. He did not do so. On the contrary, He again and again gave illustrations to show His listeners that it was a desirable condition, which would be brought about among them through the power of Spirit. He did not say that it could be attained quickly. For instance, He said: "What is the kingdom of God? And to what shall I compare it? It is like a grain of mustard seed which a man took and sowed in his own garden; and it grew and became a tree, and the birds of the air made nests in its branches."

And again, "It is like leaven which a woman took and hid in three measures of meal, till it was all leavened."

It is a great mystery how these comparisons of heaven ever came to be construed as referring in any way to a locality in the skies. What relation to a city with streets of gold has a mustard

seed, planted in the earth and springing forth
into a tree, or a little cake of yeast fermenting
a baking of bread?

A remarkably strange lot of comparisons
Jesus used, if He had in mind a place where
the good were to go after death! He never pre-
tended to convey any such meaning.

Jesus' idea of the kingdom of heaven is a
condition to be brought about in the affairs of
men, here on the earth. It is to grow from small
beginnings, like a mustard seed or the yeast
cake. His disciples were sent forth to sow the
seed in a definite way, by carrying into the
midst of men the signs that evidence the power
of Spirit, through which the kingdom of heaven
is to be established, right here on this planet.
There is no basis for any other view.

Symbolic Heaven   All the theories about
                      a place called "heav-
en" are founded on John's symbolical description of New Jerusalem, which was pictured, in
the imagination, as the fulfillment on earth of
the very movement which Jesus inaugurated and
which He described as having such small beginnings.

This city which John saw is among men.
"Behold, the dwelling of God is with men. He
will dwell with them, and they shall be his

people, and God himself shall be with them; he will wipe away every tear from their eyes, and death shall be no more, neither shall there be mourning nor crying nor pain any more, for the former things have passed away." All this describes what is to take place here among us. No reference is made to its being among angels, or to its being established at the time that John saw the vision. It is to be consummated in new conditions on earth.

If the kingdom which Jesus taught is in the skies, why did He direct His disciples to pray:

"Thy kingdom come,

Thy will be done,

On earth as it is in heaven"?

Now that men are opening up the hidden resources of nature, in earth and in air, possibilities of achievement are dawning on them, and they see that human endeavor will yet make the earth a paradise.

No one should be deluded with the vague assumption that there is a place in the skies, or on some faraway planet, called "heaven." There is not the shadow of a foundation in either the Old or the New Testament for such doctrine. On the contrary, the teaching is clear that all the heaven which men will ever find will be here. It is here now, and it will be revealed to everyone who rends the veil of sense.

At Hand   The teaching, "The kingdom of heaven is at hand," is not alone indicative of the quick ushering in of a new order of things. It states a fact of subjective consciousness in man. Nothing else is so near to man as God and the kingdom of heaven. They exist eternally in the depths of man's own unrevealed consciousness. He has them in the hidden recesses of his mind, exactly as he has the circulation of the blood in the hidden veins of his body. He is not conscious of the blood before he looks for it; and he is not conscious of God and of his own spiritual nature before he gets into the deeps of his own soul.

It is the subjective or interior consciousness that is to be made objective or exterior. To the question of His disciples as to when the kingdom of heaven would come, Jesus answered, "when the without shall become as the within" (Apoc. New Testament).

This one passage should forever settle the location of heaven. It is the *within,* and it will come to the consciousness of humanity when it is brought forth to the without, when the without conforms to its conditions.

It is the *within* which Jesus set vibrating in the minds of His disciples when He sent them forth to do the works of power. He was familiar with the inner realm, and dwelt there much of the time. This realm exists today, and may be discovered by whosoever will look for it.

Proclaiming   If the kingdom of heaven exists right here in our midst, and simply needs to be revealed to our veiled eyes, all we have to do is to proclaim the presence of the kingdom by faith and works. The way by which to make it visible will follow.

It is not alone a question of perception. The kingdom must be made manifest. All manifestation arises through action. You cannot exercise your right to be, without making manifest some of the potentialities of Being. You must use your talent. The talent of which man is possessed, surpassing all else, is that of thinking. To think is to make manifest the world of forms. Every time you hold a thought in your mind, you are forming a body for that thought; and bodies are things. A belief in matter and limitation forms a body of matter and limitation. If you want a body of freedom and light, think thoughts having at their base freedom and light. Man never rises higher in expression than his thought. His thought never rises higher than the idea back of it. If you want to rise in the scale of being, watch your ideas. From them flow your environment. Your environment is your prison wall when you are chained to the limitations of sense.

Dynamics   In the world of ideas, the metaphysician has discovered that
there is a realm having potentialities, whose
depths he has not sounded. This realm is to him
the great storehouse of wisdom and life, and he
finds that his own center of consciousness is like
it. He is essentially one with it. His thinking
faculty represents the mechanical device through
which this All-Principle is made manifest. His
word sets into motion the machinery, and results
follow in the realm of ideas in a manner paralled
with those in the realm of dynamics.

The kingdom is an internal condition first,
last, and always. The internal opening of man's
finer faculties results in an externality corresponding in degree. This externality is not to
be the guage of the existence of the kingdom of
heaven. That it is considered such, is the error
of the sense man. He is cumbered with things,
and his cry always is, "Make me happy in my
possessions, and I shall be satisfied." But this
is not the attitude of the spiritual man. His
possessions are of the soul. His pleasures are of
the mind and of the heart. Whoever has these
has at least begun the kingdom.

Larger Purpose   The wise man does not
center his attention upon
effects. They are to him as the ashes. The fire of

the original Spirit is ever new and fresh. He does not identify himself with the ashes, consequently he never has to count himself at the end of existence. Ashes are carried out, and cast to the four winds, but the fire burns on and on.

You are here for a purpose. That purpose is never fulfilled so long as you are dazed by the demands of the senses; nor are you fulfilling the law of your being by going over, day after day, the petty round of human existence.

You have been cast in a larger mold than this. God did not create you to be forever dust and ashes, to be blown about by the four winds.

Awake! sleeper in the human mind. Rise out of low ideals into the high. Rouse yourself, for the kingdom of heaven is at hand. You are a king! Bestir yourself; the Christ of God is born in you, and the hour of your reign is truly at hand!

Advanced Soul   Jesus was a very advanced soul, and His radiant body was developed in larger degree than that of anyone in our race, but we all have this body, and its development is in proportion to our spiritual culture. In Jesus this body of light glowed "as he was praying." Jesus' body did not go down to corruption, but He, by the intensity of His spiritual devotion, restored every cell to its innate state of atomic light and power.

Jesus lives today in His body of glorified electricity in a kingdom that interpenetrates the earth and its environment—the kingdom of the heavens.

Great teachers and leaders of the race have really developed and expressed a superconsciousness that is potential in all persons. When the natural world is scientifically and universally revealed, a great school of instruction in soul unfoldment will be established right here in our midst, and its results will be beyond all our present imaginings.

The mysteries of supermind have always been considered the property of certain schools of occultists and mystics who were cautious about giving their truths to the masses for fear that in their ignorance these might misuse them. Now the doors are thrown wide open, and whosoever will may enter in.

New Dimension The kingdom of the heavens, the new dimension of mind and energy, is being unfolded today in spiritual substance. It is an ideal state in creative mind, ready to be ushered into the minds of men. Its source is not in outer things. It comes from sources within men. So we must develop spiritual understanding and spiritual power. Man is the outpicturing of the infinite and creative Mind, and all the capacity of that great Mind is his by inheritance.

The Holy Spirit

THE GOSPEL is now universally identified with Jesus' mission and the doctrine that has grown out of it. When we speak of the gospel we refer to that system of religious beliefs that has centered about the teachings of Jesus of Nazareth.

As to what that gospel is in detail, there are many opinions. Many believe that it is the plan of salvation for men outlined in the dogmas and creeds of the churches. But those doctrines, creeds, and dogmas were formulated three hundred years after Jesus taught and demonstrated.

There is no authority from Him or from His immediate disciples attesting the genuineness of many of these later enunciations interpreting the original teachings. They are the work of men. These teachings are not the pure Christianity of Jesus Christ.

It is safe to assert that no one can know the doctrine of Jesus Christ without going direct to Him for information. The writings of the New Testament known in the four Gospels are the most reliable external guide. When these are studied with unbiased mind, it is perceived that Jesus delegated no ecclesiastical power to anybody. He did not formulate His doctrine or authorize any other human being to do so.

The Counselor   Jesus appointed one teacher: "The Counselor, the Holy Spirit, whom the Father will send in my name, he will teach you all things, and bring to your remembrance all that I have said to you."

The Holy Spirit is the only authorized interpreter of the gospel of Jesus Christ. No man can know what His doctrine is unless he gets it direct from this one and only custodian. It is not to come secondhand. Each for himself must receive it from the Holy Spirit, who is sent by the Father in the name of the Son.

Holy Spirit   The question is frequently asked, "Who is the Holy Spirit, and what relation does He bear to God and to Christ?"

The early disciples knew the Holy Spirit as the third person in the Trinity. The Father is always first, the Son second, and the Spirit third. The terms Father and Son express an eternal, reciprocal relation. The Spirit is the infinite "breath" of God as the Son is His infinite "Word."

We may understand the relation and office of the Father, the Son, and the Holy Spirit by analyzing our own mind and its apparent subdivisions during thought action, because each one of us is a perfect copy in miniature of the great universal first cause—Being.

The Holy Spirit is the executive power of both Father and Son, carrying out the creative plan. It is the personality of Being. It is the personality of God. It is neither the all of Being nor the fullness of Christ, but is an emanation, or breath, sent forth to do a definite work. Thus circumscribed, He may be said to take on, in a sense, the characteristics of personality, a personality transcending in its capacity the concept of the intellectual man.

The Holy Spirit is described in Scripture as personality and as not always existing for the consciousness of humanity in uniform degree. The mission of Jesus was to open the way for the Holy Spirit to enter into the minds of men.

Function   The function of the Holy Spirit, or Spirit of truth, implies distinct personal subsistence: He speaks, searches, selects, reveals, reproves, testifies, leads, comforts, distributes to every man.

The Holy Spirit is the law of God in action; in that action He appears as having individuality.

The normal condition of man is one of inner communion. It is the mission of the Holy Spirit to bring all men and all women into this inner communion. He who is buried in sense limitations must find the way out of them into the place where the light shines. It is the mission of the Holy Spirit to guide man in order that he will not mistake the way and wander into the darkness of many delusive bypaths.

The Holy Spirit comes to men in this day, as in the past, and reveals to them in various ways how to overcome the erroneous states of consciousness that they have evolved, or in which they are cast through association. A higher and more farseeing guide than mere intellect is necessary. That guide has been provided in the Holy Spirit.

The Holy Spirit is the one factor that Jesus' disciples and immediate followers counted absolutely necessary to their success in preaching the gospel of Jesus Christ. They looked to Him for power and guidance in all their work. They announced Him as the special gift promised by Jesus, an endowment that could be given by them to those who believed on His name.

By the laying on of hands they transferred Holy Spirit power to others, who upon receiving it went about preaching, teaching, prophesying, and healing.

Availability   The Holy Spirit is in the world today with great power and wisdom, ready to be poured out upon all those who look to Him for guidance. The Holy Spirit is authority on the gospel of Jesus Christ. He is the only authority ever recognized by Jesus Christ, and whoever attempts to set forth the Christ gospel from any other standpoint is in the letter and not in the Spirit.

Jesus gave His words into the keeping of this universal receptive agency, the Spirit of truth, whose mission it is to carry those words directly into the understanding of everyone who accepts the Christ way into the kingdom of heaven.

The Holy Spirit gave His words to the

writers of the New Testament, and they wrote
them out for the comprehension of the intellectual man. This does not signify that the mission
of the Holy Spirit ended there—that after giving this message He then withdrew from the
world. On the contrary, it was just the beginning, the primary step of that larger, more comprehensive teaching that Spirit is ever ready to
impart to every soul.

The soul needs instruction. The Father has
provided a perfect way for us to get it. That way
is the Jesus Christ way. Whoever follows the
steps outlined in the gospel, now brought to
each of us by the Holy Spirit, will finally reach
the same place that Jesus reached.

Shortcoming of Language

Everyone has
a soul to save,
not from the hypothetical hell after death, but
from the sin and the delusions of the sense consciousness that make hell here and now. There
is a way to bring that salvation about. It is the
mission of the Holy Spirit to reveal that way to
every one of us.

The revelation begins the moment we turn
from the letter of the gospel and seek for its
spirit. To know that every word and sentence
of Scripture veils a spiritual truth is the first
step in unraveling the gospel. Spiritual truths

cannot be expressed in language that will carry correct concepts to the mind. No attempt to describe the Holy Spirit is made in Scripture, because language might be expanded indefinitely, description and illustration fill volumes. The Holy Spirit would not be compassed or apprehended on the intellectual plane where human language passes current. The Holy Spirit is the whole Spirit of God. He can be known by man only through his spiritual nature. When he tries to bring Spirit down to the plane of things, he always falls short.

So those who attempt to learn of the Holy Spirit by reading about Him, or from the teachings of others, will fail. The Holy Spirit comes only to those who earnestly seek Him. If you are depending for spiritual enlightenment on some book or on church ritual and doctrine or on some teacher or leader, you need not expect to have the Holy Spirit fall upon you. It is the prayer of the soul alone in its upper room that brings the Holy Spirit.

The Interpreter   The doctrine of Jesus Christ is so intimately associated with the Holy Spirit that they are inseparable. The Holy Spirit is the interpreter of the Christ, and the Christ is the thing interpreted. They are omnipresent and cannot be separated in spirit or in works. Hence, to preach the gospel of Jesus Christ is to set forth that the Holy Spirit of God is ready and willing to bring all men and all women into the kingdom.

All down the ages it was assumed that the requirements are met when men have been persuaded to believe in the Lord Jesus Christ as the Savior of their souls, and to keep believing this until they pass out of their bodies; then, the teaching runs, believers are received into the arms of the Lord. But the Holy Spirit does not endorse this assumption, neither does the letter of the Scriptures.

Open Door   Jesus opened the door of unity with the Father to all who believe on Him. It is thought by nearly everybody that Jesus was the only Son of God. Jesus wants companions in power, dominion, and glory, that it may be demonstrated to the world, this world, that what He claimed about his relation to God is true.

The gospel of Jesus Christ is that all men shall become God incarnate. It is not alone a gospel of right living. It shows the way into dominion and power equal to and surpassing that of Jesus of Nazareth. If we have a sense of inferiority, if we believe that He has greater wisdom, or power, or love, then we are not fulfilling the requirements. So long as we feel any difference between ourself in the Father and Jesus in the Father, we have fallen short of that "mind . . . which you have in Christ Jesus."

The cry goes up: "This is foolish, sacrilegious, to put man beside Jesus Christ and claim that they are equals." The claim is not that humans, in their present consciousness, are equal with Jesus, but that they must be equal with Him before they will emerge from the sense of delusion in which they now wander.

Health Is Normal   We know that health is the normal condition of man and that it is a condition true to his real being. We claim and declare this truth right in the face of appearances to the contrary. We have proved by experience many times repeated that our words in this way reveal that health is potential in Being.

If man is the son of God, he must be that son right now. Sonship must be just as real, just as omnipresent, as the health that God has revealed through His Word. How shall man reveal his sonship to himself and to others except by claiming it? He does so by declaring that he is not a son of mortality, but a son of God, and that the Spirit of God dwells in him and is now shining through him.

Your word is the power through which you make your belief manifest. Simple belief in or assent to the truth of a proposition never gave understanding to anyone. There must be mental action. Organic changes in the mind are necessary before the new state of consciousness takes up its abode in you.

If you can convince yourself that you are a son of God, your next step is to declare it in word and to carry it out in the acts of your daily life. After declaring this, if you fall short in demonstrating yourself to be a son of God, you are to find out why. You have neglected some of your spiritual powers. You may be dissipating the energy given you by the Father.

Mission   Here is the mission of the Holy Spirit. When you ask in the silence of Spirit to be shown why you do not manifest the power that Jesus of Nazareth manifested, the Holy Spirit will in some way reveal to you the lack. How that revealment will come about no one can tell you. But if you are patient and trustful you will be guided and directed so that all the links in the chain of your being will be brought together and harmoniously joined, and the Son of God will be revealed in you.

Baptism

IN THE regeneration two states of mind are
constantly at work. First comes the cleansing
or denial state, in which all the error thoughts
are eliminated. This includes forgiveness for
sin committed and a general clearing up of the
whole consciousness. The idea is to get back
into the pure, natural consciousness of Spirit.
This state of mind is typified by John the Baptist, who came out of the wilderness a child of
nature whose mission it was to make straight the

way of One who was to follow. In the first baptism, through the power of the word, the sense man is erased from consciousness, and the mind is purged and made ready for the second baptism.

Second Baptism   Putting away of sin from the consciousness (baptism through denial, plus forgiveness) is very closely allied to the deeper work that is to follow; so much so that to the observer it seems the same. Hence the followers of John, when they saw the works he did, asked if he was the Messiah. His answer was that the One who followed him was to baptize with the Holy Spirit.

In the second baptism, the creative law of divine affirmation, set into action by Mind, lights its fires at the center of man's being, and when thus kindled raises soul and body to a high degree of purity. This process is known as regeneration.

From this we discern that mental cleansing and the reforms that put the conscious mind in order are designed to prepare the way for that larger and more permanent consciousness which is to follow. This is the denial of "self" or personality. We are all guilty in a way of undue devotion to personal aims, which are always narrow and selfish. So long as these exist and

take the place of the rightful One there is no
room for the higher self, the Christ of God.

Holy Spirit   The baptism of the Holy Spir-
                     it is a quickening of the spiri-
tual nature that is reflected in mind and body.
Spiritual baptism has power. It is affirmative. It
is positive. This outpouring of the Holy Spirit
is the second baptism. It is the most precious
gift of God and comes to those who steadfastly
seek first the kingdom of God and His righteousness.

The recorded "This is the Son of God" is a
reference to a matter of first importance in the
regeneration. The recognition of man as the Son
of God and the establishment in the mind of
the new relations between the divine Father and
the Son are essential to the process. If we do
not affirm our sonship, with all its privileges
and powers, we are sure to belittle ourself and
make limitations that prevent us from entering
into the fullness of the Godhead.

John the Baptist   Metaphysically inter-
                        preted, John the Bap-
tist symbolizes in each individual the natural
man, but with an illumined intellect. His face is
turned toward the light in the measure that he
recognizes and pays homage to the higher self

within the individual. John baptized with water all those who believed that Jesus was soon to make His appearance. This is a cleansing, purifying process, preparing the individual to see spiritually and to discern spiritually.

By cultivation the spiritual mind becomes an active factor in consciousness. It has to be desired and sought before it becomes a part of one's conscious life. The natural conscious mind is expecting, looking for, and earnestly desiring a greater realization of Spirit. He knows that he is not fulfilling the Christ ideal of manhood. Willingness to give up the natural man to the divine is a most propitious sign in one who is in the regenerative process. Many persons are ambitious to put on Christ, but are not willing to give up the present man in order to do so. This mind has no personal ambition. It is innocent, loving, and obedient to the call of God.

Zeal   Never neglect your soul. To grow spiritually you should exercise your zeal in spiritual ways. As children of God our place is at the right hand of the Father. When man really realizes this, he calls down upon himself the baptism of the Holy Spirit. He soon learns that obedience to Spirit increases his power to control his thoughts and thus make his world conform to the divine standard.

When man is obedient to Spirit he will not suffer burdens. To trust Spirit he must know of its guidance by experience. For those who have not learned the guidance of Spirit, that experience must be acquired. Man is spirit and must find himself before he can communicate with universal Spirit.

Materiality We are pressed upon by beliefs in materiality. Thoughts make things. The material beliefs that are pressing upon us are just as substantial in the realm of mind as material things are substantial in the realm of matter. Everything has origin in thought, and material thoughts will bring forth material things. So you should baptize and cleanse yourself totally with your spiritual word. When the baptizing power of the word is poured out, it cleanses all material thought. Impotence is vitalized with new life, and the whole subconsciousness is awakened and quickened.

Man does not exercise the power of his spiritual nature, because he lacks understanding of its character and of his relation to the originating Mind in which he exists. From Divine Mind man inherits power over the forces of his mind—in truth, power over all ideas. A quickening from on high must precede man's realization of his innate control of thought and feeling. The baptism of the Holy Spirit is a quickening of the spiritual nature, which is reflected in intellect and in body. When one understands the science of Being, one is prepared to receive this baptism and to utilize it along deeper lines of thought. Power is essential to the work that Jesus Christ expects His followers to do in the great field of humanity. Man should apply the power of the word to his individual redemption, and he should speak the redeeming word of Spirit to the multitudinous thought people of his own soul and body.

Transcendent Wisdom   There is in man a knowing capacity transcending intellectual knowledge. Nearly everyone has at some time touched this hidden wisdom and has been more or less astonished at its revelations. It certainly is a most startling experience to find ourself giving forth logical thoughts and words without preparation or forethought, because we nearly always arrive at our conclusions through a process of reasoning. However, this reasoning process is often so swift that we are likely to think that it is true inspiration, especially when we have received either the reflected uplift of other wise ones or the baptism of the Holy Spirit. This quickening of the intellect is intellectual illumination that precedes the awakening of the ideal, the Christ understanding. Some Truth students become so enamored of the revelations they receive through the head that they fail to go on to the unfoldment of the One who baptizes "with the Holy Spirit and with fire."

Intellectual Understanding Intellectual understanding of Truth, as given in the first baptism, is a tremendous step in advance of sense consciousness. Its possession brings a temptation to use for selfish ends the wisdom and the power thereby revealed. When Jesus received this baptism He was "led up by the Spirit into the wilderness to be tempted by the devil" (personal ego) before he could take the next degree in Son-of-God consciousness.

Jesus knew that the illumination of the personal is not the fulfillment of the law. He rejected every temptation to use His understanding for selfish ends. Unless the disciple is very meek he will find the human ego strongly asserting its arguments for the application of the power of Spirit to personal needs. The god of mammon is bidding high for men who have received the baptism of Spirit. Many sell out, but their end is dust and ashes. No man can serve two masters.

Voice of Spirit   When we discover in ourself a flow of thought that seems to have been evolved independently of the reasoning process, we are often puzzled about its origin and its safety as a guide. In its beginnings this seemingly strange source of knowledge is often turned aside as a daydream. Again it seems a distant voice, an echo of something that we have heard and forgotten. One should give attention to this unusual and usually faint whispering of Spirit in man. It is not of the intellect and it does not originate in the skull. It is the development, in man, of a greater capacity to know himself and to understand the purpose of creation.

Understanding is opened in both head and heart when man gives himself wholly to the Lord. Both receive the baptism of Spirit. Man receives first an intellectual understanding of Truth which he transmits to his heart, where love is awakened. The Lord reveals to him that love is the greatest power in man.

If you are living in your thinking faculty intellectually, if you believe in birth and death, you must come out of that belief. You are not exercising your rightful dominion, but are subject to error thought. When the thinking faculty is obedient and does what it is told, it is always rewarded.

Your Place You are Spirit, the Son of God, and your place is at the right hand of the Father. To realize this is to call down upon yourself the baptism of the Holy Spirit, after which baptism you no longer labor, but begin to gather together your powers of mind. This gathering together of your powers is an orderly process.

There is an ever-present, all-knowing One. Put yourself into conscious unity with this presence through the power of your thought and your word, and you will gradually become mentally open to a world of causes of which you never before dreamed.

Atonement

W E HAVE been taught that Jesus died for us—as an atonement for our sins. By human sense this belief has been materialized into a flesh-and-blood process, in which the death of the body on the Cross played the important part. Herein has the sense consciousness led us astray. That spiritual things must be spiritually discerned seems to have escaped notice in forming the scheme of atonement. At the root of the teaching is Truth.

Jesus of Nazareth played an important part in opening the way for every one of us into the

Father's kingdom. However, that way was not through His death on the Cross, but through His overcoming death.

To comprehend the atonement requires a deeper insight into creative processes than the average man and the average woman have attained; not because they lack the ability to understand, but because they have submerged their thinking power in a grosser thought stratum. So only those who study Being from the standpoint of pure mind can ever understand the atonement and the part that Jesus played in opening the way for humanity into the glory which was theirs before the world was formed.

Overcoming Jesus must have been the product of a former cycle of time, and He had previously made the perfect union in the invisible with the Father.

In proportion as people understand and have faith in Jesus their actual Savior from sin, and in proportion as they are set free from appetite, passion, jealousy, prejudice, and all selfishness, they experience wholeness of mind and body as the result.

The ultimate result of this knowledge and of daily practice in overcoming will be a new race that will demonstrate eternal life—the lifting up of the whole man, spirit, soul, and body

—into the Christ consciousness of oneness with the Father. This is indeed true glorification. By means of the reconciliation, glorification, and at-one-ment that Jesus reestablished between God and man we can regain our original estate as sons of God here upon earth.

Sanctification   When we have found our being in God, we are no longer identified with the world; our interest is in spiritual things. Through our intense realization of the eternal good and our unity with it we become so saturated with the thought of good that we are impregnable to evil. Thus we find that the doctrine of sanctification is based on Truth. It is possible for us to become so good in purpose that everything we do will turn to good.

We must certainly sanctify ourself in Christ and persistently send forth the word of purity and unselfishness to every faculty in order to demonstrate it.

The realization of divine unity is the highest that we can attain. This is true glory, the blending and merging of the whole being into Divine Mind.

When a soul makes complete union with God-Mind there is always an outpouring of the Holy Spirit upon it. This is true glorification, the acknowledgment by the Father that the Son is indeed lifted up.

Realization means at-one-ment, completion, perfection, wholeness, repose, resting in God. A realization of health brings to the consciousness an inner knowing that the divine law has been fulfilled in thought and act. Then as man lays hold of the indwelling Christ he is raised out of the Adam or dark consciousness into the Christ consciousness. This at-one-ment with God brings a lasting joy that cannot be taken away.

Christ Consciousness Jesus was more than a man of Nazareth, more than any other man who ever lived on the earth. He was more than man, as we understand the appellation in its everyday use, because there came into His manhood a factor to which most men are strangers. This factor was the Christ consciousness.

The unfoldment of this consciousness by Jesus made Him God incarnate, because Christ is the Mind of God individualized. Whoever so loses his personality as to be swallowed up in God become Christ Jesus or God-man.

We cannot separate Jesus Christ from God, or tell where man leaves off and God begins in Him. To say that Jesus Christ was a man as we are men is not correct, because He had dropped

that personal consciousness by which we separate ourselves into men and women. He was
consciously one with the absolute principle of
Being. He had no consciousness separate from
that Being, hence He was that Being to all in-
tents and purposes. He attained no more than is
expected of each of us.

It is all accomplished through the externali-
zation of the Christ consciousness, which is
omnipresent and ever ready to manifest itself
through us as it did through Jesus.

Accomplishment   This principle has been
                        perceived by the spiri-
tually wise of every age. They have not known
how to externalize it and to make it an abiding
state of consciousness. Jesus accomplished this
and His method is worthy of our adoption because, as far as we know, it is the only method
that has been successful. It is set forth in the
New Testament. Whoever adopts the life of
purity and love and power exemplified in the
experiences of Jesus of Nazareth will in due
course attain the place that He attained.

The way to do this is the way Jesus did it.
He acknowledged Himself to be the Son of
God. The attainment of the Christ consciousness calls for nothing less on our part than a
definite recognition of ourselves as sons of God

right here and now, regardless of appearances to the contrary. We know that we are sons of God—then why not acknowledge it and proceed to take possession of our God right? That is what Jesus did in the face of most adverse conditions. Conditions today are not so stolidly material as they were in Jesus' time. People now know more about themselves and their relation to God. They are familiar with thought processes and how an idea held in mind will make itself manifest in the body and in affairs; hence they take up this problem of spiritual realization under most favorable conditions.

It must work out just as surely as a mathematical problem, because it is under immutable law. The factors are all in our possession and the rule that was demonstrated in one striking instance is before us. By following that rule and doing, day by day, the work that comes to us, we shall surely put on Christ as fully and completely as did Jesus of Nazareth.

Impersonal   Be thankful that God is no respecter of persons, that Truth cannot be revealed by one mortal to another. God is a special, personal Father to every one of His children, and from no other source can they get Truth.

Jesus Christ clearly revealed the Father in

His consciousness. He points the way. Believe and keep His sayings, and follow Him. By adopting His methods you will find the same place in the Father that He found.

Transfiguration

TRANSFIGURATION is always preceded by a change of mind. Our beliefs must be lifted from the material, the physical, to the spiritual. But first we need to realize that it is possible for us to be transfigured as well as to understand the law by which transfiguration is brought about.

The meaning of the Transfiguration has never been understood by those who read the Scriptures as history. The Transfiguration of Jesus has always been considered a historical event, and its allegorical meaning overlooked.

To get the real meaning of the Transfiguration, we must regard the experience of Jesus on the Mount as typical of what often takes place in those who are growing in spiritual consciousness.

Evidences   We have evidences every day of the power of thought to transfigure the countenance. We know that it is possible for a person to be transformed in a degree by the thoughts that flit through his mind from moment to moment, but we do not know his capacity for transfiguration, which is unlimited, nor the part it plays in his attainment of the Christ consciousness and the Christ body.

The real object of existence is to bring forth the perfect man and attain eternal life. Eternal life must be earned. It is usually assumed that man does not die, and this is true of the I AM; but how about the consciousness, the soul? "The soul that sins shall die" is the testimony of the Scriptures. That only lives which conforms to the principle of eternal life.

Consciousness   Spirit exists eternally in God-Mind, of which we must become conscious. This consciousness is soul and is the tangible part of soul. God-Mind gives us the opportunity to incorporate into our soul or consciousness His attributes. These attributes are spiritual life, love, wisdom, strength, power, in fact the essence of all good, which we realize first in the mind, then in body and affairs. Thus God gives us the spiritual perfection that we are to manifest and retain eternally in consciousness. This is His Son or Christ.

Jesus taught that we must attain the consciousness of eternal life, that we have no life in us until we have attained this consciousness. Until we demonstrate over death, the death of the body, we are in a transitory state of existence.

Realization   The real object of existence is
                      to attain the consciousness of
eternal life and to manifest all that is potentially involved in us by our Creator. The Spirit—I AM or ego—in man is eternal, but there must be a consciousness of this quality of eternity; there must be a consciousness of the image-and-likeness man.

There must be in every one of us a realization of that Spirit which has in it—involved in its being—all that exists in the universal. If we do not realize this, if we do not make it ours, we must eventually go back to the universal. Jesus was the great Way-Shower to the attainment of this realization of Spirit. We shall miss "the

prize of the upward call" if we do not enter the
path that He trod and that He pointed out in
many parables, illustrations, and experiences.

The overcoming or lifting up of man is a
process through which we are all passing if we
have been converted to the Christ way of life.
Transfiguration plays a part (and an important
part) in this evolution of the soul. When we
see the parallel between our experiences and the
Transfiguration of Jesus we gain confidence to
go forward.

Three Virtues   In our study and applica-
                         tion of the Christian life
we all have times when we are spiritually up-
lifted. Such a time is marked by a form of
spiritual enthusiasm, which is brought about by
statements of Truth made by ourself or others
—prayers, words of praise, songs, meditations—
any statement of Truth that exalts the spiritual
realms of the mind. Jesus was lifted up by Peter,
James, and John (faith, judgment, and love).
Whenever we dwell upon these virtues and try
to live up to them, they are exalted in consciousness, and they go up with us to the Mount of
Transfiguration. You may not always realize
this. You may think that the uplifting was just
a passing exaltation, but it stamps itself upon
your soul and body and marks the planting of

a new idea in the upward trend of the whole man.

What is your attitude toward these times when you feel the mighty uplift of Spirit? Do you give them their due importance; or when you again come down into the valley, do you groan and question and wonder why you do not abide in your exaltation, why there seems a falling away of the mind from it?

Essential Unity Right here we must be wise and understand the relation of the higher principles of man and their action in the redemption of soul and body. Do not lose sight of the fact that the whole man must be spiritualized. Some people get into the habit of going up in spirit to the Mount of Transfiguration, and they find it so enticing that they refuse to descend to the valley again. Then soul and body are left to go their own way, and a separation ensues. Such persons dwell continually on the heights and ignore the essential unity of spirit, soul, and body. Many delusions arise among Christians because they lack understanding of the law of the idea and its manifestations. All things, all actions, all principles, are working toward the unity of God, man, and the universe. But there must be a readjustment and a cleansing of the whole mass.

If there are things, whether mental or physical, that are not up to the high standard of Spirit, they must die. Jesus on the Mount spoke of His death which was to follow. This death is of the material perception of substance and life, which is reflected in man's body of flesh. This must perish. The limited concept of matter and of a material body must be transformed so that the true spiritual body may appear.

Salvation   Some teach the saving of the soul and the perishing of the body. Jesus taught the saving of both soul and body. It is true that this mortal body must be transfigured. It is but a picture or symbol of the real, the spiritual body, which is the "Lord's body." The "Lord's body" is the body of Spirit, the divine idea of a perfect human body. When one realizes this new body, the cells of the present body will form on new planes of consciousness. They will aggregate around new centers, and the "Lord's body" will appear.

When the body is devitalized by excessive labor, dissipation, or any loss of vital force, its aura shrinks away and a consciousness akin to that of being unclothed is evident. When the mind is adjusted to the divine law, all the vital forces flow harmoniously and the aura glows about the body as a beautiful white light, protecting it from all discord from without and purifying it continually from within.

True prayer brings about an exalted radiation of energy. The word of Truth bursts forth in a stream of light that, when held in mind, illumines, uplifts, and glorifies.

Fulfillment

JESUS Christ was the product of a cycle of human development that was before our present cycle of development. We revel in speculating about the history of His soul's unfoldment and the true reason why He was so far in advance of our time.

When the soul of the race became involved in the pleasures of sensation and sought other guidance than that of Jehovah God, gradual degeneration of the whole human family began until men were in a bad way. Something had to be done. Someway, somehow we had to be lifted out of the murky darkness of sense thought. Jesus Christ provided and provides today the greatest impetus to the ongoing of our race.

Scientific understanding of His great truths thrills the soul with the desire for spiritual attainment, with a longing for spiritual fulfillment. Many persons proudly acknowledge Him and claim His promises.

When here on earth, through His mastery of spiritual laws of which we today have only an inkling, He performed many seeming miracles. Think of the condition in those times of a body that had been dead for four days! Imagine Jesus thanking God that His petition had been heard and then speaking the word of life to one who had lain in the grave for this length of time. Then imagine this person instantly being charged with new life. Imagine great streams of life flowing through his every cell and fiber until he came walking out of the tomb, restored to perfect health. Imagine Jesus in the consciousness of perfect unity with God speaking the healing word to many "sick unto death" and each one instantly throwing off the disease and coming forward sound and well.

Upliftment   To lift the race out of sense thought Jesus was compelled by the necessity of soul sympathy to become an intimate associate of the people. He sought to help. Hence He incarnated into the race and was "in every respect tempted as we are, yet without sinning." He revealed that we are children of the same Father as He. He is our Elder Brother, our helper. We are His people, and He is interested in our progress.

Jesus proclaimed: "I am the light of the world." "You are the light of the world." When He spoke thus He was speaking of this inner light which gives life and intelligence to all creation.

The development of spiritual light is the destiny of us all. We shall not be satisfied until we "awake in His likeness." All are radiant in a certain degree with this spiritual light, but especially those who have an understanding of Spirit and its universality. We feel the light and sometimes mentally see it flashing into expression when we have a spiritual uplift gained from a new idea of Truth. Some feel its influence and are moved to higher things by it; or if it is radiating gloomily, they are moved to depression and discouragement.

Transfusion   Through Jesus' experience on the Cross, where His precious blood was spilled, through His suffering there He lowered His consciousness to the consciousness of the race, thereby administering to the whole race a blood transfusion, imparting to both the soul and the body of men the properties of Being that will restore man to his divine estate. Thus, we are on the way to fulfillment and the Jesus Christ way!

Jesus Christ broadcast the electrons of His blood into the race thought atmosphere and they may be apprehended by all who believe in Him. These electrons become centers of energy and life in those who appropriate them. Thus, men gradually transform and regenerate their blood and their body. This is the real spiritual meaning of being saved by Jesus Christ. The blood is the life. Jesus really came to bring to the whole human family a larger consciousness of life.

Life is a universal energy that moves even the corpuscles of the blood. Therefore life is more powerful than the blood. Consequently we believe that it was through the "shedding," the getting rid, of the idea of flesh and blood that Jesus accomplished His great works. He tapped the great reservoir of divine life and raised His consciousness of life to that of the Father.

The Lord's Supper The Lord's Supper is God's covenant with mankind, through His perfect idea, Christ Jesus. This compact was completed through Jesus' breaking the bread and blessing the cup. The bread symbolizes spiritual substance, or the body, and we drink His blood by affirming and realizing our oneness with the one divine, omnipresent life of Spirit.

Through Jesus Christ we all have access to this perpetual life stream. We must really eat of His substance, as He taught us; that is, we must appropriate it as spiritually ours. We must drink of His blood: let His life stream flow through our mind and body, healing, cleansing, and purifying us in every way. This is the grand at-one-ment of man's life and with the life of God through Jesus Christ. This is the way to perfect fulfillment.

Now   The man who wants the inner life to spring forth must believe in the reality of the omnipresent spiritual life and must exercise his faith by invoking in prayer the presence of the invisible but omnipresent God. This reveals to consciousness the glory of Spirit, and the soul has witness of itself of a power that it knew not.

In Spirit all things are fulfilled now. The moment a concept enters the mind, the thing conceived is consummated through the law that

governs the action of ideas. The spiritual-
minded take advantage of this law and affirm
the completeness of this ideal, regardless of
outer appearances. This stimulates the energy
in the thought process and gives it power beyond estimate.

I AM Action   The soul in conscious touch
                        with the Father-Mind and
striving to fulfill the divine law brings the
power of true words to bear in the purifying
cleansing of its faculties. The necessity of abiding in the I AM in order to bear much fruit is
affirmed. When our faith attaches itself to outer
things, instead of the spiritual I AM, it ceases to
draw vitality from the one and only source of
life, divine Principle.

The only door to this life is the I AM. This
abiding is a conscious centering of the mind in
the depths within us by means of repeated affirmations of our faith and trust in it. This day-
by-day repeating of affirmations finally opens a
channel of intelligent communication with the
silent forces at the depths of Being; thoughts
and words flow forth from there, and an entirely new source of power is developed in the
man.

When the thought or "word" of Truth from
the supreme I AM of consciousness becomes an

abiding fact in our mind, we need no longer strive in external ways. We have but to express a deep desire in the soul and it is fulfilled.

Sabbath   The consciousness that we have fulfilled the divine law in both thought and act is the Sabbath. It has nothing to do with any day of the week. God did not make days and weeks, nor has He darkened His clear concepts of Truth by the element of time. Time is an invention of the human.

The true Sabbath is that state of mind in which we rest from outer thought and doings, and give ourselves up to meditation or to the study of things spiritual. It is when we enter into the stillness of our inner consciousness, think about God and His law, and commune with Him. It is a state of mind that man enters or acquires when he goes into the silence of his own soul, into the realm of Spirit. There he finds true rest and peace, a perfect stage of one's spiritual unfoldment.

Reincarnation

THE Western world in general looks upon reembodiment, or reincarnation, as a heathen doctrine. Many people close the door of their minds upon it, without waiting to find out what message it brings when interpreted in the light of Truth. It is the object of this presentation to set forth the Unity teaching concerning reincarnation; to show why we consider it reasonable, and to explain its relation to, and its place in, the Christ doctrine.

Jesus Christ Teaching   The teaching of Jesus Christ is that all men shall, through Him, be made free from sin and be saved to the uttermost—spirit, soul, body. Until this salvation is attained, there is death. To give men opportunity to get the full benefit of salvation, life is necessary. A body through which to express is also necessary. When man loses his body by death, the law of expression works within him for reembodiment. He takes advantage of the Adam method of generation to regain a body. Divine mercy permits this process in order that man may have further opportunity to demonstrate Christ life.

Regeneration   Generation and death must give place to regeneration and eternal life. The necessity of rebirth must therefore pass away with all other make-shifts of the mortal man. It will have no place when men take advantage of the redeeming, regenerating life of Jesus Christ and quit dying.

Reembodiment should not be given undue importance. It is merely a temporary remedy to be followed by the real, which is resurrection. The whole man—spirit, soul, and body—must be lifted up into the Christ consciousness of life and perfection.

Heathen Thought   Whenever there has been a nation of thinkers who were not bound in materialism, those thinkers have accepted reembodiment as a fact. It is rejected only where the craze for wealth and for fame and for the things of the world has darkened the mind with materiality.

The heathen who have not received Truth as revealed by Jesus Christ do not know where and how reembodiment fits into the race redemption. To them it is a fixed, unalterable law.

They believe in karma, the accumulated effects of the sins of past lives. The burden of karma they have carried for ages, and they expect to carry it for ages more until they have worked out of it. This makes them victims of a blind fatalism, weary treadmill travelers from birth to death, and from death to birth.

There is no such hopeless note in the doctrine of Jesus Christ. He came to bring a full consciousness of abundant life, complete forgiveness and redemption from all sin, victory over death and the grave, so delivering man from any occasion for reembodiment and from all beliefs of karma.

The heathen hold that reincarnation is one of the natural evolutionary steps of man's development. We teach, and our doctrine is sustained by the teachings of Jesus, that rebirth is the unifying force of nature at work in its effect to restore man to his original deathless estate. Man, through his disregard of the law of life, brought death upon soul and body. A single span of life, from the birth of an infant to the death of an old man, does not constitute all man's opportunity for life.

Continuity   Life is continuous and in harmony with the wholeness of Being only when it is expressed in a perfect body; hence man must have a body in order to gain an abiding consciousness of life. Through repeated trials at living, man is finding out that he must learn to control the issues of life. The divine law, as taught by Jesus Christ, must be understood and applied in all life's details, and when this is done the Eden state will be restored.

The objections that the natural man raises to reembodiment arise largely from the fact that he lives in the personal consciousness and cannot see things in the universal. He thinks that by reembodiment he loses his identity. But identity endures. Personal consciousness does not endure. The personal man is not immortal and he dies. This is clear to anyone who is willing to give up his belief in the reality and importance of the personal consciousness.

Release   All the personal man—his limitations, his relations—must give

way to the universal, the Christ. The privilege
is ours to give up or forsake everything—father,
mother, wife, children, houses, lands—for
Christ's sake, and so enter into the consciousness of the absolute. By doing this we come into
the realization of eternal life and receive a
hundredfold more than we have forsaken.

If we refuse and cling to the old family relationships, there is nothing for it but to meet
the result of our choice, and to give all those
relations up by death. It is just a question of
giving up a little for the all and of gaining
eternal life. So if reembodiment frees one from
the old personal relationships, it is not such a
dreadful thing after all. It cannot give anything
more than new personal relations. Rising out of
these into the universal is a work that everyone
must do willingly for himself. Death and reembodiment do not give redemption. Reincarnation serves only as a further opportunity to
lay hold of redemption.

Union   The pure, incorruptible substance
of Spirit, built by the transforming
power of the Christ into the organism through
true, pure, spiritual thought and word, makes
the body incorruptible and eternal. As the mind
changes from error to Truth, corresponding
changes take place in the body, and the ulti-

mate of these changes is perfection and wholeness in every part. Therefore those who are trying to lay hold of eternal life have ground for
their faith in the promise that they will be
saved from the grave.

Knowing that spirit, soul, and body are all
necessary to man and that he cannot truly be
said to live except in their conscious union and
expression, the error of believing that death is
the open door to a higher life, the gateway to
heaven, is easily seen. There is no progress in
death. Death is negation. The demonstration of
eternal life can be made only in life—soul and
body together working out the problem and together being lifted up.

Mortal Mind   The idea of progress in
                       death has its origin in the
mortal mind, which reasons from its own limitations instead of from absolute Truth. The
mortal mind desires to preserve eternally the
personal consciousness and all personal relations. Man therefore attempts to make and to
people a heaven, or spirit world, where all the
old family relations are as he knows them in his
present life. He clings to this belief with a
tenacity worthy of a better object, and it is usually only after hard experience that he is willing to drop the personal. Eternal life cannot be

demonstrated in personal consciousness. The great family of Jesus Christ, the redeemed Adam race, are all one, and the little selfish relationships of the Adam man have no place in the new order.

Illogical Beliefs Another illogical belief about the destiny of man is that the patriarchs and the prophets, and all others who have lived, have been lying in their graves, some of them for thousands of years, having no place in the onward movement of the race.

Another teaching, unfounded in Scripture or in reason, holds that they who formerly lived are now either in a realm of eternal bliss or in a state of unending torment. It is far more logical to believe that the race is a unit and that all its members grow and develop together as well as individually. Thus we find it only reasonable to think of every man and every woman as coming onto the stage repeatedly, keeping up connection with the race and its experiences.

Growth Mortal consciousness has no power to lift itself out of ignorance and sin, so the mere matter of repeated births has not taken the race forward. It is the descent of Spirit from time to time, as the people have

been able to receive it, that has made all progress. As man's growth has made it possible, new
truths have been discerned and new dispensa-
tions have come. When the time was ripe, Jesus
came and brought the good news of salvation
from death. His words had to work in the race
consciousness for nearly two thousand years before anyone was sufficiently awakened and
quickened to believe in a complete redemption
and to strive to lay hold of it. The promise is
that the leaven of the Word will finally leaven
the whole of the human family and that all will
come into the light of life.

From the standpoint of the universal it is
plain that reembodiment serves a purpose in
affording opportunities for spiritual development. All that is gained in spiritual growth in
one life experience becomes part of man's real
identity. If he is faithful, he will finally gather
such a store of spiritual power and wisdom that
he can demonstrate salvation of his body through
Christ. But reincarnation is only an opportunity.

Resurrection   If generation and reincarna-
                        tion are not the means of
restoring to their place in the race those who
have died, what is the means that accords with
the divine law? Resurrection.

Whether they still walk the earth, or have

ceased to breathe and have been buried from sight, all are in a dead state, and all must be raised from the grave of ignorance and sin. Right now the resurrection work is going on. Men and women are awakening to a new consciousness of life, of understanding, and of bodily perfection. This resurrection work must extend to every member of the Adam race, whether he is what we call alive or whether he, as Jesus said of the dead, sleeps. All must be awakened and be unified in soul and body.

Many of the present-day beliefs about resurrection have come down from past centuries of ignorance, and have been accepted without question. They seem to be a literal interpretation of certain Bible texts. In these, as in all Scripture, we must get back of the letter and see the spiritual meaning of the parables and the symbols used to teach the truth about the raising of the dead. As we do this we find going on in ourself the very awakening and resurrection that we once supposed would come in a single day to buried people. When this raising up, redeeming process has gone far enough in us, we shall probably be the means of awakening and raising other buried ones.

Phases Everyone begins where he left off. When reembodied, he has opportunity to come up into Jesus Christ, identify himself with the Jesus Christ race, and demonstrate through Him the deathless life. We must remember that there are steps and phases in this great process. When we understand them, we shall see that men will be raised to their place in the Adam race, then raised out of Adam into Christ.

Everyone who would demonstrate that he is risen with Christ must first lay hold of life by faith and affirm, without wavering, that he is raised out of sin and condemnation and death into life eternal. Then the word of life carries on, day by day, the resurrecting, redemptive work in the mind and in the body. Every day some old limitation or error loses its hold and passes away, and the imperishable, incorruptible substance of Truth becomes a little more firmly established in consciousness. In this way the body is transformed and raised up in honor, incorruptible, immortal.

It is not profitable to allow our mind to dwell upon mortal questionings about how the work of Spirit is to be done in and through us. It is our place to hold ourself in a positive life thought, realizing always the omnipresence and perfection of life in God, thus bringing perfect life more and more into manifestation in ourself and in others. When we realize how much our faithfulness means to the race, we shall rejoice in being true to the great truths that will bring to pass the time when death and the grave will be no more.

Memory   That you do not remember your past lives proves nothing. Neither do you remember the day on which you were born, but you do not on that account question the fact of your birth. Comparatively little of your present life is remembered. But that does not alter the fact that you have lived. Memory, to the natural man, is a matter of physical brain records, photographic or phonographic in character. The memories of experiences in past lives are not clearly recorded in the new brain structure of the infant. Such memories are usually in the nature of vague impressions. The sense of identity is blurred.

In the book of life, the great Mind of the universe, all identity is sharply marked. As the individual becomes quickened and raised out of personal consciousness into the universal, he will be able to bridge over the breaks in personal experience. He will come to himself. Realizing his spiritual identity as the son of God, he will not entangle himself with either present or past personality, but will claim and demonstrate his divine sonship. He will no longer limit himself in a brief span of life, beginning with birth and ending with death, but will live in the consciousness of eternal life, which has neither end nor beginning.

Treatments for Self-Development

Treatment to Realize God

There is one Presence, one Intelligence, one Substance, one Life: the good omnipotent. God is the name of the everywhere present Principle.

Thy name is Spirit. I know Thee as the one all-seeing Mind.

Treatment to Realize Spiritual Sonship

I am the son of God, and the Spirit of the Most High dwells in me. I am the only begotten son, dwelling in the bosom of the Father. I am the Christ of God. I am the beloved son in whom the Father is well pleased. He that hath seen me hath seen the Father. I and my Father are one. I am the image and likeness of God, in whom is my perfection. All that the Father has is mine.

Thou art always with me as indwelling wisdom and love. Thy law is now the standard of my life, and I am at peace. Thou art never absent from me. I dwell in Thee and share Thine omnipotence. In Thee is my perfection.

Treatment to Know the Truth

God is Truth. The Truth is: God is Principle, Law, Being, Mind, Spirit, All-Good, omnipotent, omniscient, omnipresent, unchangeable, Creator, Father, Cause, and Source of all that is. God is individually formed in consciousness in each of us, and is known to us as "Father" when we recognize Him within us as our Creator, as our mind, as our life, as our very being. Mind has ideas and ideas have expression. All manifestation in our world is the result of the ideas that we are holding in mind and are expressing. To bring forth or to manifest the harmony of Divine Mind, or the "kingdom of heaven," all our beliefs must be one with divine ideas, and must be expressed in the divine order of Divine Mind.

Treatment to Realize the Spiritual Ideal

My highest ideal is a perfect man. My next highest ideal is that I am that perfect man. I am identity demonstrated. My perfection is now established in Divine Mind. I am one with Almightiness. Through Christ I have dominion over my every thought and word. Of a truth I am the son of God.

Treatment to Realize Perfect Manifestation

My "life is hid with Christ in God." I am the substance of Being made manifest. I am formed in the perfection of the divine-idea man, Christ Jesus. My body is the temple of the living God, and the glory of the Lord fills the temple. My body is not material; it is spiritual and perfect in all its being. By seeing perfection in all things, I help to make it manifest. I see in mind that perfect character which I desire to be.

Treatment to Realize Light

The glory of the Lord is risen upon me, and I walk in the light of life. Christ within me is my glory. The brightness of His presence casts out all the darkness of error, and my whole body is full of light. My understanding is illumined by Spirit.

Treatment to Develop One's Viewpoint

The Christ of God is born in my consciousness, and I am glorified in my understanding. My understanding is established in Divine Mind. My spirit is quickened in Christ. I know the reality back of the shadows. I see the light of the Christ consciousness always. I see perfection in all forms and shapes.

Treatment for Right Thinking

With my mind's eye I see more and more the reality of the true ideas ever existing in divine principle. I firmly believe in the guiding Intelligence that directs all my thoughts. I am in authority, I say to this thought, " 'Go,' and he goes, and to another, 'Come,' and he comes." Where my thoughts are gathered together in my Christ name, there I am in the midst of them.

I will think no evil, for Thou art always with me. I think Thy thoughts after Thee.

Treatment to Realize Freedom

God is good, and God is all; therefore I refuse to believe in the reality of evil in any of its forms. God is life, and God is all; therefore I refuse to believe in the reality of loss of life, or death. God is power and strength, and God is all; therefore I refuse to believe in inefficiency and weakness. God is wisdom, and God is all; therefore I refuse to believe in ignorance. God is spiritual substance, and God is all; therefore there is no reality in the limitations of matter. God is inexhaustible resource, and God is all; therefore I refuse to believe in the reality of lack or poverty. God is love, and God is all; therefore I refuse to believe in hate or revenge.

Treatment to Realize Substance

I believe in the presence and power of the one Mind, and it is to me substantial intelligence. Holding continuously to the reality of things spiritual establishes them in mind—they become mental substance. My mind is opened anew to the splendor of God's kingdom, and a flood of rich substance now pours itself into my affairs.

Treatment to Develop Faith

The understanding of Spirit clarifies my faith. My faith is of God and in God. My faith grows greater day by day, because it is planted in Truth, and through it the mountains of mortal error are moved into the sea of nothingness. My doubts and fears are dissolved and dissipated; in confidence and peace I rest in God's unchangeable law. My faith comprehends the beauty of wholeness. I am persuaded that God is able, that He is willing, that He is eager to give me whatsoever I ask.

Treatment to Develop the Body

My body does not starve for my love and appreciation of it. I recognize it, honor it, and love it as the body temple of the living God. I have now the only body I ever had. Though I were reincarnated a thousand times, yet is my body the same. It is I. Its appearance depends upon my beliefs and thoughts and changes accordingly, but it is always the same body, even as my soul and spirit are always the same. My body is as much a part of my individuality as my soul. It is eternal, like any other part of my I. It is I, even as my soul is I. My body came from no one but God. It came from Him with my spirit and soul and has ever coexisted with them. These three are one, inseparable. I do not own my body: I am body. I do not own my soul: I am soul. I do not own my spirit: I am spirit. These three are one. I am. I am in every cell of my body. I am every cell of my body. I do not disown my body. I do not withdraw my I, but I take possession—full possession—of every part in the name of the Lord. My body is life, purity, wholeness, sinlessness. In my flesh I see God. What I see, what I behold, becomes manifest.

Denial Treatment for Well-Being

I deny that I inherit any belief that in any way limits me in health, virtue, intelligence, or power to do good. Those with whom I associate can no longer make me believe that I am a poor worm of the dust. The race belief that "nature dominates man" no longer holds me in bondage, and I am now free from every belief that might in any way interfere with my perfect expression of health, wealth, peace, prosperity, and perfect satisfaction in every department of life. By my all-powerful word, in the sign and presence of Almighty God, I now unformulate and destroy every foolish and ignorant assumption that might impede my march to perfection. My word is the measure of my power. I have spoken, and it shall be so.

Affirmation Treatment for Well-Being

I am unlimited in my power, and I have increasing health, strength, life, love, wisdom, boldness, freedom, charity, and meekness, now and forever. I am now in harmony with the Father, and stronger than any mortal law. I know my birthright in pure Being, and I boldly assert my perfect freedom. In this knowledge I am enduring, pure, peaceful, and happy. I am dignified and definite, yet meek and lowly, in all that I think and do. I am one with and I now fully manifest vigorous life, wisdom, and spiritual understanding. I am one with and I now fully manifest love, charity, justice, kindness, and generosity. I am one with and I now fully manifest infinite goodness and mercy. Peace floweth like a river through my mind, and I thank Thee, O God, that I am one with Thee!

The Sevenfold Cleansing of the Temple

The eye represents the discerning capacity of the mind.

My eyes are no longer darkened by thought of deception, concealment, or lust. The cleansing life and light of Spirit make pure and clean these eyes, and through all-seeing Mind I have spiritual vision.

The ear represents the receptive capacity of the mind.

My ears are no longer stopped by the sensitiveness and willfullness of the little self. I am no longer bound by personality. I now bathe in the great ocean of life, and I am free in boundless Spirit. I hear the voice of Truth only and rejoice.

The nose represents the initiative capacity of the mind.

The cleansing life of Spirit frees my mind of all thoughts of fear, timidity, and incapacity. I am bold, free, courageous Spirit, and I can do all things through Christ.

The tongue represents the judging capacity of the mind.

Sense appetite no longer clogs the clear discernment of my spiritual judgment. The cleansing life of Spirit quickens and cleanses my taste, and I eat and drink only what my body requires under divine law.

Feeling represents the loving capacity of the mind.

I am no longer in bondage to the thought that sensation is in matter. The cleansing life of Spirit dissolves all fleshly lust for sense pleasure. I am Spirit, and I desire the clean, pure currents of life to flow through every part of my body, so that all may be made clean.

Intuition is the natural knowing capacity of the mind.

The cleansing life of Spirit purifies my heart, and I trust the "still small voice" within my soul.

Telepathy is thought interchange.

The cleansing life of Spirit clears my mind of ignorance and materiality, and I see the activity of ideas and understand their import independently of human language. As God gave Daniel "learning and skill in all letters and wisdom, and . . . understanding in all visions and dreams," so He gives me and all His children the original ideas of His great mind to use as we will.

Treatment to Develop Prosperity

Infinite wisdom guides me, divine love prospers me, and I am successful in everything I undertake. In quietness and confidence I affirm the drawing power of divine love as my magnet of constantly increasing supply. I have unbounded faith in the omnipresent substance increasing and multiplying at my word of plenty, plenty, plenty. I trust the universal Spirit of prosperity in all my affairs. I come to God because I believe that He is and that He is a rewarder of them that seek after Him. I give freely and fearlessly, fulfilling the law of giving and receiving. Divine love, through me, blesses and multiplies this offering.

Father, I thank Thee for unlimited increase in mind, money, and affairs.

Golden Snowflakes

Behold, what God hath wrought!
An ideal man, a mighty man—
A man supreme, who thought by thought
Must demonstrate what God hath wrought.

Hard experiences come into our life because
we do not know the law of harmonious thinking.

All economic, social, and personal trouble
can be traced back to selfishness.

One who tries to establish self-control through will power and suppression never accomplishes permanent results.

Time is the measure that man gives to passing events.

There is but one way to establish harmony in the home, and that is to establish it first in the individual.

No one has the right to dictate what another shall do.

The cause of all accidents lies in sense consciousness. To be free from all accidents, we must raise our consciousness, so that it is spiritually positive and Christlike. Then we shall attract only good.

The greatest disintegrating element in human consciousness is resistance.

Instead of giving up to circumstances and outer events we should remember that we are all very close to a kingdom of mind that would make us always happy and successful if we would cultivate it and make it and its laws a vital part of our life.

Man is a duality in seeming only. He
is a unit when he knows himself.

The belief that God makes men do certain
things cannot be true in a single instance, because, if it were, man would not be a free agent.

God has chosen each of us as a medium
for the expression of Himself.

There are times when it is to our own spiritual
benefit and to God's glory to keep things con-
cealed and, like Mary, to ponder them in our
heart until due time for expression.

Christianity is the science of eternal life.

The great object of man's existence in planetary
consciousness is to build a body after the ideals
given by the Lord.

Our consciousness is our real environment.

God is not jealous as men count jealousy, but
He is jealous of principle, from which no lapses
are tolerated.

It is the law of Spirit that we must be that
which we would draw to us.

Spiritual beauty is the loveliness of God beheld
in His creations by the eye of man.

Cause and effect are the balance wheel of the universe.

Marriage should be a perpetual feast of love, and so it would be if the laws of love were observed.

No one ever attained spiritual consciousness without striving for it.

One must give up personal attachments before one can receive the universal.

A wish is a superficial expression of desire, and is only fleeting.

Instead of fighting modern science the new Christianity welcomes its discoveries as proofs of the veritable existence of the kingdom of the heavens that Jesus taught so persistently.

Any system that suppresses the will is radically wrong.

The soul is progressive. It must go forward. It must meet and overcome its limitations.

The buoyancy and joy of youth should be cultivated enthusiastically as the years advance.

All food is primarily mental, and in the process of digestion and assimiliation it becomes part of the body structure, making cells like itself in character.

Seeming failure is often a steppingstone to something higher.

Restlessness cannot be satisfied by change of climate or environment or by travel or by any other outward change. Only by man's finding his center in God can restlessness and discontent be satisfied.

In order to realize Truth and to demonstrate it you must live it.

Every adverse situation can be used as a spur to urge one to greater exertion and the ultimate attainment of some ideal that has lain dormant in the subconsciousness.

Every man who accomplishes things sees first in his mind what he wishes to do.

What you now comprehend is not the ultimate of your ability in any direction.

About the Author

Charles Fillmore was an innovative thinker, a pioneer in metaphysical thought at a time when most religious thought in America was entirely orthodox. He was a lifelong advocate of the open, inquiring mind, and he took pride in keeping abreast of the latest scientific and educational discoveries and theories. Many years ago he wrote, "What you think today may not be the measure for your thought tomorrow"; and it seems likely that were he to compile this book today, he might use different metaphors, different scientific references, and so on.

Truth is changeless. Those who knew Charles Fillmore best believe that he would like to be able to rephrase some of his observations for today's readers, thus giving them the added effectiveness of contemporary thought. But the ideas themselves—the core of Charles Fillmore's writings—are as timeless now (and will be tomorrow) as when they were first published.

Charles Fillmore was born on an Indian reservation just outside the town of St. Cloud, Minnesota, on August 22, 1854. He made his transition on July 5, 1948, at Unity Village, Missouri, at the age of 93. To get a sense of history, when Charles was eleven,

Abraham Lincoln was assassinated; when Charles died, Harry Truman was President.

With his wife Myrtle, Charles Fillmore founded the Unity movement and Silent Unity, the international prayer ministry that publishes *Daily Word*. Charles and Myrtle built the worldwide organization that continues their work today, Unity School of Christianity. Through Unity School's ministries of prayer, education, and publishing, millions of people around the world are finding the teachings of Truth discovered and practiced by Charles and Myrtle Fillmore.

Charles Fillmore was a spiritual pioneer whose impact has yet to be assessed. No lesser leaders than Dr. Norman Vincent Peale and Dr. Emmet Fox were profoundly influenced by him. Dr. Peale borrowed his catchphrase of *positive thinking* from Charles Fillmore. Emmet Fox was so affected by Fillmore's ideas that he changed his profession. From an engineer, he became the well-known writer and speaker.

Charles Fillmore—author, teacher, metaphysician, practical mystic, husband, father, spiritual leader, visionary—has left a legacy that continues to impact the lives of millions of people. By his fruits, he is continuously known.

Printed U.S.A.   138-1704-5M-8-95